THE
MIRACLE BERRY
DIET COOKBOOK

THE
MIRACLE BERRY
DIET COOKBOOK

Homaro Cantu

GALLERY BOOKS

New York London Toronto Sydney New Delhi

Gallery Books
A Division of Simon & Schuster, Inc.
1230 Avenue of the Americas
New York, NY 10020

First Gallery Books hardcover edition January 2013

GALLERY BOOKS and colophon are registered trademarks of Simon & Schuster, Inc.

For information about special discounts for bulk purchases,
please contact Simon & Schuster Special Sales at 1-866-506-1949 or business@simonandschuster.com.

The Simon & Schuster Speakers Bureau can bring authors to your live event. For more information or to book an event contact the Simon & Schuster Speakers Bureau at 1-866-248-3049 or visit our website at www.simonspeakers.com.

Designed by Davina Mock-Maniscalco
Miracle berry illustration by Jason Snyder
All photography © Mike Ruggirello

Manufactured in the United States of America

10   9   8   7   6   5   4   3   2   1

Library of Congress Cataloging-in-Publication Data
Cantu, Homaro
    The miracle berry diet cookbook / by Homaro Cantu.—First Gallery Books hardcover edition.
        pages cm.—(Gallery original nonfiction hardcover)
    World-renowned chef and restaurateur has created a whole new world of no-sugar dishes using miracle berries.
    1. Cooking (Berries) I. Title.
    TX813.B4C36 2013
    641.6'47—dc23
                                                                        2012028892
ISBN 978-1-4516-2558-5
ISBN 978-1-4516-2560-8 (ebook)

To Katie, who makes everything taste better

CONTENTS

Introduction   1

Breakfast   9

Muffins and Quick Breads   35

Starters   49

Mains and Sides   67

Desserts   109

Jams, Sauces, and Frostings   249

Flavor-Tripping Cocktails   271

Acknowledgments   287

Index   291

INTRODUCTION

rowing up in poverty, my access to good and healthy food was virtually nonexistent. My meals consisted primarily of school lunch or government-issued food from food pantries. It was a no-brainer that my first job at age twelve would be at a restaurant—I no longer had to worry about having enough to eat and I quickly learned that restaurants usually had good food.

I was eating better for sure, but it was more than that: I simply loved being in a kitchen and learning from more experienced chefs. The more I ate, the more voracious my appetite became. I started questioning why certain flavor combinations worked and others didn't, and did a lot of trial and error with my own unique combinations. This inevitably led me to question the science behind the techniques.

I worked in restaurants all through middle and high school. I slung burgers, worked a tandoori oven, made paella at a tapas place, and cooked for the masses at a high-volume fish house, and I loved it all.

So when I graduated from Western Culinary Institute, I spent the next three years working my way through several cities and working for free at more than fifty restaurants while also working at full-time restaurant jobs to support myself. It was an incredible experience, and I was lucky enough to learn from some of the great chefs who shaped fine dining in America as we know it today.

I worked as a baker, a pastry chef, and at every facet of savory food, eventually working my way up to the position of sous chef at Charlie Trotter's in Chicago. After four years there, I opened my own restaurant, Moto, which has been written up in over two thousand articles in more than forty countries. I've been on the *Rolling Stone* Hot List, and was once my own category on *Jeopardy!*. I've competed on—and won—*Iron Chef America*. I've appeared on dozens of television shows around the world, and was fortunate enough in 2010 to land a television series, *Future Food*, with my pastry chef and friend, Ben Roche. I'm not saying that I've seen everything in my years, but after cooking in professional kitchens for more than twenty years, consulting with NASA, pharmaceutical companies, and Fortune 500 companies, I have never experienced anything as exciting as the miracle berry.

Most people haven't even heard of the miracle berry. I learned of it about six years ago when a friend of mine asked me to help her create something for her friend who was undergoing chemotherapy and had lost her appetite. She complained of a metallic and sometimes rubbery taste in her mouth. Paula, my friend, who was also a professional chef and foodie (and one of the nicest people I know) suggested I research the miracle berry.

Ben Roche, pastry chef at Moto and one of the most creative minds on the planet, started working with me to research flavor-altering ingredients and spent weeks chewing on tin foil and tasting all kinds of foods, including miracle berries. The miracle berries actually neutralized the metallic taste in foods.

Miracle berries are a completely organic, all-natural, non-GMO (genetically modified organism) plant that contains an active glycoprotein called miraculin. When eaten, miraculin temporarily binds to your taste receptors to block your ability to taste sour flavors and alters many other flavors in food, especially spicy, salty, and bitter.

The miracle berry, aptly named, could change the future of food. If used properly, it could significantly reduce the need for refined sugar and all processed and artificial sweeteners. It could help patients actually enjoy food again, or feed the world on wild vegetation in any growing zone around the world. Yet no one has successfully created a set of real-life recipes for every day.

I started eating everything I could find with the berry. Some things tasted amazing; other things, not so good. I wanted to learn everything I could about this product and how to use it, but there was no information out there about it, and definitely no recipes. So I spent the next year cooking with them, tasting everything before and after eating a miracle berry.

Finally, I started to incorporate miracle berries into various courses at Moto restaurant. The response from our customers was so overwhelming, we decided to build another, more casual restaurant next door to Moto, called iNG (Imagining New Gastronomy) to introduce the miracle berry to a much wider audience. At first, we only offered it at the chef's table in our kitchen called the Flavor-Tripping Table. Within three weeks of opening, the demand for this one table was so high, that we made this the only option at iNG. Imagine how much fun it would be to order a drink that tastes like a gin and tonic, and then, after eating a miracle berry, turns into a Sloe Gin Screw. That's one of our flavor-tripping cocktails. I knew we were on to something more than just fun when diners wanted to talk about the possibilities of eliminating sugar from their diet with these berries and about their interest in getting them to try at home.

In my restaurants, I am constantly trying to change the way people eat—the menu is edible, the candle on your table actually becomes a sauce for a dish, we even serve a dish that looks like a lit cigar with edible ash. My goal is to give diners something unexpected and, I hope, unforgettable. Innovation is the most important part of my professional life, without question. Without it, food becomes stagnant and positive change takes a back seat.

Like most chefs, I have always dreamed of writing my own cookbook, but the reality is that what I do at Moto restaurant, such as using cutting-edge technologies like class IV lasers and liquid nitrogen to prepare food, is not something most home cooks would ever do. I wanted to create a book that could spark a positive shift in eating at home.

As a dad of two young daughters, I worry about their future and health. I worry about what they consume and what is hidden in their everyday foods. I think about my dream to change the world and think, "Why can't positive social change be fun and entertaining? Could it start with something as simple as a berry?" Working on this book has been a true labor of love for me. When you try the recipes in this book, I promise you it will be unlike any food experience you have ever had, and I hope it will change your life.

Where to Get Miracle Berries

Miracle berries can be purchased in a few different forms. My favorite way to enjoy the berry is in its tablet form. It's the most consistent product and has the longest shelf life because the berries are freeze-dried and formed into tablets with a small amount of cornstarch for binding. Outside of growing your own berries, tablets are also the most cost-effective way to buy them. You can even cut a tablet in half for a smaller amount. It is important to understand that once opened, the tablets are highly perishable and should be kept tightly wrapped in an airtight container and stored in a cool, dry place away from your stove.

I purchase my tablets from a website, www.mberry.us, but they are also available at other places online. You can purchase freeze-dried or frozen whole berries. For freeze-dried whole berries, follow the same storage procedure as the tablets. For the frozen berries, make sure not to thaw them unless you plan on consuming them immediately. When you do decide to eat the frozen berries, just allow them to come to room temperature for twenty minutes and refrigerate for no more than a day. If you are eating a whole berry, don't eat the pit—it's pretty bitter. Finally, you can grow your own plants. I am a fairly well-rounded gardener and I must warn you that growing these yourself can be a challenge. They require a tropical environment and highly acidic soil for the best possible product. Talk to the grower who creates the plant and see how much success they have had in getting their plants to bear fruit; keep in mind that even the most skilled growers will not see fruit until the plant is three to four years old, and only 50 percent of all plants will bear fruit. Once you get a plant to fruit, then you can expect crops twice a year with as many as four hundred berries per plant—perhaps enough for a single person to use this book every day and eliminate sugar from their diet.

Getting Started

Assuming you have a miracle berry tablet, suck on it like a cough drop. Do not chew it. Let it dissolve so it coats all areas of your mouth. This will take about three minutes. If you have the whole berry, simply remove the seed in the center and immediately consume the berry.

Raid your refrigerator and taste some of these ingredients that illustrate the miraculous effect it has on different foods:

- LEMON. It will taste like lemonade, the best lemonade you've ever tasted. Squeeze some lemon juice into soda water—it's delicious and calorie free.

- LIME. It will taste like a lime that is as sweet as an orange. The best orange you've ever tasted. I have watched people eat an entire lime after eating a miracle berry.

- TOMATO. Even the most flavorless, unripe tomato will taste sweet and perfectly ripe.

- GRANNY SMITH APPLE. The tartness is still there, but the apple taste sweeter, which makes a great flavor combination.

- BANANA tastes more tropical, as if there are more layers of flavor—notes of passion fruit or pineapple.

- PINEAPPLE tastes like pure candy.

- STRAWBERRY. Even the most unripe strawberry bursts with sweetness.

- TAMARIND is just as sweet, but not puckery tart.

- HOT SAUCE. You can actually taste the peppers and layers of flavors, not just the heat.

- HOT PEPPER. The spices are slightly subdued, and the pepper tastes sweeter and more floral.

- SWEET PEPPER. Even the most average pepper will taste like the sweetest, ripest pepper you have ever eaten.

- COFFEE. Squeeze a little lemon juice into hot or cold coffee. No need for those pink or yellow packets!

Are you hooked? Can you imagine miracle berry's effect on things you eat every day? The flavor altering effects of miracle berries last approximately thirty to forty-five minutes, depending on the person, which is the average time most people take to eat a meal. We've created these recipes specifically to work with the properties of the miracle berries, so make each recipe exactly as it appears in the book and enjoy the recipes within thirty to forty minutes after consuming a miracle berry or tablet.

I need to clarify that even though this book has the word "diet" in the title, I am not a dietician and don't claim to be a nutritional expert. I simply wanted to minimize the amount of refined sugar and synthetic sugar substitutes in desserts. In my nondietician opinion, eating foods that taste sweet without those harmful ingredients is a healthier approach—and sometimes it takes an unconventional approach to solve complex problems.

Another important point about this book is the use of agave nectar. Sugar does a lot more in recipes than add sweetness: it's what makes baked goods tender or crisp, adding texture, and of course promotes browning. I've used agave nectar in many recipes to recreate the texture, tenderness, and browning while relying on various acids to add sweetness. Agave nectar is widely available at grocery stores in the organic food section as well as online. The nectar comes from the agave plant that is also used in making tequila. It has a much lower glycemic index than honey or refined sugar, and so it can be safer, with moderate use, for diabetics. Remember that, particularly if you are diabetic or have other health issues, you should consult your doctor before introducing agave nectar into your diet—or any other new food or substance. The flavor of agave nectar is sweet with a natural clean finish. When we calculate the amount of calories saved, we use the following formula: we total all of the sugar removed from the recipe, let's say it adds up to 200 calories. But then we add back 50 calories of agave nectar for structure. That means that we have saved 150 calories in that recipe.

At Moto, I am always stressing to my cooks that the most important part of cooking is seasoning your food. Without seasoning, food is bland and just not exciting. All tasty foods are seasoned to one degree or another, which usually means salt. The recipes in this book are seasoned with acidic products like lemons, limes, grapefruits and vinegars, as well bitter ingredients. I encourage you to try these products alone and become very familiar with them while eating a miracle berry.

In my restaurants we are lucky to be able to use the best products from around the world. We fly seafood in fresh from both coasts, produce is always local, and even our flour is hand milled. When using the miracle berry, even imperfect ingredients taste almost perfect.

My wife and I love to cook and eat together (of course!). We have been using the miracle berries in savory foods and cocktails for years, so we have developed a collection of recipes we like to make for family and friends, and we've tweaked them over the years to make them more family friendly now that we have two little critics at home.

The recipes in this book are based on those, eliminating refined sugar wherever possible and trying to keep as healthy as possible without sacrificing flavor. When possible, we've calculated the number of calories saved by simply eliminating sugar or making a substitute with honey or other natural ingredients. Hope you enjoy them as we do and we hope this book empowers you to eliminate sugar from your diet.

BREAKFAST

Amazing Overnight Waffles

MAKES 6 SERVINGS

You have to plan ahead for these, but it's really easy to whip up the batter the night before and cook in the morning. The first time I tasted one of these waffles, I couldn't believe how crisp and light they were compared to even the best regular waffles. They are well worth the extra planning and are simply divine, even plain. The sweetness comes from the sour fermentation of the yeast, which works amazingly well with the miracle berry.

Ingredients

2 cups skim milk

One ¼-ounce package active dry yeast (2 ¼ teaspoons)

½ cup warm water (100 degrees F)

8 tablespoons (1 stick) unsalted butter, melted

1 teaspoon salt

1 tablespoon honey

3 cups sifted unbleached all-purpose flour

2 large eggs, slightly beaten

½ teaspoon baking soda

Canola oil spray

Directions

Warm the milk in a small saucepan until it bubbles. Remove from heat.

In a small bowl, dissolve the yeast in 100 degrees F water. Let stand until creamy, about 10 minutes. After 10 minutes, if you do not see any bubble activity, the water was too hot and killed the yeast. If this is the case, start over with the proper temperature of water, which should be 100 degrees F.

In a very large bowl, combine the milk, yeast mixture, butter, salt, honey, and flour. Mix thoroughly with an electric mixer until the batter is smooth. Make sure to scrape the sides and bottom of the bowl with a rubber spatula to ensure even incorporation of all the ingredients. Cover with plastic wrap and let stand at room temperature overnight on top of a baking sheet in case of a spillover.

The next morning, heat a waffle iron according to the manufacturer's instructions. If not serving the waffles as soon as each is cooked, preheat the oven to 200 degrees F.

Stir the eggs and baking soda into the batter. Beat well. Spray a bit of canola oil on the waffle iron grids. Pour the recommended amount of batter into the waffle iron. Close the waffle iron and cook until golden brown; don't peek until it's done. Serve hot or place on a baking sheet in a single layer to keep warm in the oven.

When you are ready to eat, let the miracle berry tablet dissolve on your tongue and then enjoy the dish.

---

*Replacing 9 tablespoons of sugar with 1 tablespoon of honey
and the sweetness from the berry saves 61 calories per serving.
Replacing traditional syrup with our Raspberry Syrup (see page 24)
saves an additional 60 calories per serving, for a total of 121 calories saved per serving.*

Orange Waffles

MAKES 3 SERVINGS

Yes, these are called "orange waffles" even though there is no orange in the recipe. That is because the miracle berry sweetens the lime juice and makes it taste like orange. A perfectly sweet orange waffle is the result.

Ingredients

2 cups unbleached all-purpose flour

4 teaspoons baking powder

½ teaspoon salt

2 large eggs, separated

1 cup skim milk

½ cup freshly squeezed lime juice

6 tablespoons (¾ stick) unsalted butter, melted

Canola oil spray

Cherry Compote (page 166), for serving

Directions

Heat a waffle iron according to the manufacturer's instructions. If not serving the waffles as soon as each is cooked, preheat the oven to 200 degrees F.

In a bowl, mix the flour, baking powder, and salt. In a separate bowl, beat the egg whites until soft peaks form. In third bowl, beat the egg yolks, milk, lime juice, and butter. Whisk in the flour mixture, making sure to break up most of the lumps. Gently fold in the egg whites, one-third at a time, to keep the batter as light and airy as possible.

Spray a bit of canola oil on the waffle iron grids. Pour in the recommended amount of batter. Close the waffle iron and cook until golden brown; don't peek until it's done.

Serve hot, or place on a baking sheet in a single layer to keep warm in the oven. Serve with cherry compote.

When you are ready to eat, let the miracle berry tablet dissolve on your tongue and then enjoy the dish.

Replacing 2 tablespoons of sugar with the sweetness from the berry saves 32 calories per serving. Using our Cherry Compote instead of traditional cherry compote saves an additional 77 calories, for a total of 109 calories saved per serving.

Dreamsicle Crepes

These crepes are totally addictive. The sweetness that comes from the lemons, limes, and nonfat sour cream is simply perfect.

Crepes

1 cup unbleached all-purpose flour

Pinch of salt

3 eggs

2 cups skim milk

Juice of 1 lemon

Juice of 1 orange

Canola oil spray

Dreamsicle Filling

2 lemons

2 oranges

2 limes

1 cup nonfat sour cream

Directions

TO MAKE THE CREPES: In a large bowl, whisk together the flour and salt. In a separate bowl, beat the eggs. Stir in the milk, lemon juice, and orange juice. Gradually add the liquid ingredients to the flour, stirring until combined. Refrigerate for 1 hour.

TO MAKE THE FILLING: Squeeze the juice from 1 of the lemons, 1 of the oranges, and 1 of the limes; reserve the mixed juices. For each remaining fruit, slice off the top and bottom from the fruit. With a paring knife, cut downward from the top to remove the peel and white pith. Cut between the membranes to loosen the sections of fruit. Squeeze any remaining juice from the membranes of each fruit and add to the reserved juices. Combine fruit sections and juice with sour cream.

Spray a nonstick skillet with canola oil. Ladle ¼ cup of batter into pan, tilting the pan with a circular motion so the batter coats the bottom of pan evenly.

Cook each crepe for about 2 minutes, until the bottom is light brown. Using your fingers or a spatula, turn and cook the other side for about a minute. Place 2 tablespoons of the filling in the center of each crepe and fold the crepe into fourths or roll them up and serve.

When you are ready to eat, let the miracle berry tablet to dissolve on your tongue and then enjoy the dish.

Replacing ⅔ cup of sugar from the crepe filling
with the sweetness from the berry saves 102 calories per serving.

Spiced Pumpkin Pancakes

MAKES 16 PANCAKES (8 SERVINGS)

These pancakes have the most satisfying melt-in-your-mouth consistency. When I first started experimenting with miracle berries at work, I made these for a staff meal—the chefs couldn't believe they were sugar-free. Here we use cider vinegar as the sweetener with the miracle berry to create a full-flavor pancake.

Ingredients

1 ½ cups skim milk

2 tablespoons agave nectar

1 cup canned 100% pure pumpkin
   puree

1 large egg

2 tablespoons vegetable oil

2 tablespoons apple cider vinegar

2 cups unbleached all-purpose flour

2 teaspoons baking powder

1 teaspoon baking soda

1 teaspoon ground allspice

1 teaspoon ground ginger

1 teaspoon ground cinnamon

½ teaspoon salt

Canola oil spray

Toasted walnuts (optional)

Lemon wedges (optional)

Directions

In a large bowl, combine the milk, agave nectar, pumpkin, egg, oil, and vinegar. In a separate bowl, combine the flour, baking powder, baking soda, allspice, ginger, cinnamon, and salt. Add to the pumpkin mixture, stirring only enough to combine.

If not serving the pancakes as soon as they are cooked, preheat the oven to 200 degrees F. Lightly spray a griddle or heavy skillet with canola oil and heat over medium-high heat. The surface is hot enough when a few drops of water sprinkled on it dance and disappear.

Pour ¼ cup of the batter onto the griddle for each pancake. Turn when bubbles appear on the top of the pancake and edges look dry. Brown the other side, about 2 minutes more, and serve hot, or place on a baking sheet in a single layer to keep warm in the oven. Serve with the walnuts and a squeeze of lemon juice, if desired.

When you are ready to eat, let the miracle berry tablet dissolve on your tongue and then enjoy the dish.

Replacing ½ cup of sugar with 2 tablespoons of agave nectar and the sweetness from the berry saves 33 calories per serving.

Blueberry Pancakes

MAKES 8 PANCAKES (4 SERVINGS)

There is just something special about a Saturday morning that starts with pancakes. My daughters were destined to love these pancakes because my wife insisted on these daily during both her pregnancies—with blueberries, raspberries, or blackberries.

Ingredients

2 large egg whites

1 cup skim milk

Juice of 1 lemon

1 ¼ cups sifted cake flour (see note)

1 tablespoon baking soda

½ teaspoon salt

Pinch of ground nutmeg

Pinch of ground cinnamon

Canola oil spray

½ cup fresh blueberries
  (or any fresh berries)

Directions

In a large bowl, whisk the egg whites till fluffy. Add milk and lemon juice. Stir. Gently mix in flour, baking soda, salt, cinnamon, and nutmeg. Stir, but do not overmix. Let batter sit for about 5 minutes.

If not serving the pancakes as soon as they are cooked, preheat the oven to 200 degrees F. Lightly spray a griddle or heavy skillet with canola oil and heat over medium-high heat.

The surface is hot enough when a few drops of water sprinkled on it dance and disappear.

Add berries to the batter and fold gently to combine, making sure to break apart as few berries as possible. Pour ¼ cup of batter at a time onto hot griddle or pan. Turn when bubbles appear on the top of the pancake and edges look dry. Cook another minute. Serve hot or place on a baking sheet in a single layer to keep warm in the oven.

NOTE: If you don't have cake flour, you can make your own. For every cup of cake flour needed, place 2 tablespoons of cornstarch in a 1-cup measure, then fill the rest of the cup with all-purpose flour. Sift the ingredients a few times to aerate the mixture.

When you are ready to eat, let the miracle berry tablet dissolve on your tongue and then enjoy the dish.

—————————

Replacing 2 tablespoons of sugar with the sweetness from the berry saves 24 calories per serving. Replacing conventional syrup with our Raspberry Syrup (see page 24) saves an additional 60 calories per serving, for a total of 84 calories saved per serving.

Puffed Apple Pancake

In this recipe, I use Golden Delicious apples. However, Granny Smiths will also work, as they have higher acidity and taste sweeter with miracle berries. Additional sweetness comes from the cider vinegar, a natural fit with apples.

Ingredients

¾ cup skim milk

4 large eggs

¼ cup apple cider vinegar

2 tablespoons agave nectar

1 teaspoon pure vanilla extract

½ teaspoon salt

¼ teaspoon ground cinnamon

⅔ cup unbleached all-purpose flour

4 tablespoons (½ stick) unsalted
butter

2 Golden Delicious apples, peeled,
cored, and thinly sliced

1 teaspoon ground nutmeg

Lemon wedges, for serving

Directions

Preheat the oven to 425 degrees F.

Whisk the milk, eggs, vinegar, agave nectar, vanilla, salt, and cinnamon in large bowl until well blended. Add the flour and whisk until the batter is smooth.

Place the butter in 13 by 9-inch glass baking dish. Place dish in the oven until butter melts, about 5 minutes. Remove from the oven and arrange the apple slices in overlapping rows in the baking dish. Return to the oven and bake until apples begin to soften slightly and the butter is bubbling and beginning to brown around edges of dish, about 10 minutes.

Pour the batter over the apples. Bake until the pancake is puffed and brown, about 20 minutes. Sprinkle with the nutmeg and a squeeze of lemon juice and serve.

When you are ready to eat, let the miracle berry tablet dissolve on your tongue and then enjoy the dish.

Replacing ¼ cup of sugar with 2 tablespoons of agave nectar and the sweetness
from the berry saves 18 calories per serving. Replacing conventional syrup
with our Raspberry Syrup (see page 24) saves an additional 60 calories per serving,
for a total of 78 calories saved per serving.

French Toast

Mmmm . . . French toast. I'll admit it, I love anything that's fried. But it's especially good when it's a good-quality piece of bread fried until it's crisp on the outside with a custard-like soft middle. For this recipe, we replace sprinkling powdered sugar with sweetness gained from the lemon juice.

Ingredients

6 large eggs

¼ cup skim milk

2 tablespoons freshly squeezed
  orange juice

2 tablespoons freshly squeezed
  lemon juice

1 tablespoon honey

1 teaspoon ground cinnamon

¼ teaspoon ground nutmeg

Pinch of salt

Pinch of ground cloves

1 tablespoon unsalted butter

1 tablespoon vegetable oil

Eight ¾-inch-thick slices whole-grain
  bread (preferably day-old or stale)

Directions

In a large shallow baking pan, beat the eggs. Stir in the milk, orange juice, lemon juice, honey, cinnamon, nutmeg, salt, and cloves. Mix until well combined.

Heat the butter and oil in a large skillet over high heat until hot. Working with as many slices as your skillet will hold at one time, dip the bread into the egg mixture and soak for 30 seconds. Lift out the bread slices, allowing the excess egg mixture to drip off, and place in the pan. Turn down the heat slightly and cook until browned and crisp, about a minute or two. Turn and cook the other side for another minute or two. Serve immediately.

When you are ready to eat, let the miracle berry tablet dissolve on your tongue and then enjoy the dish.

Replacing ¼ cup of sugar with 1 tablespoon of honey and the sweetness from the berry saves 32 calories per serving. Replacing conventional syrup with our Raspberry Syrup (see page 24) saves an additional 60 calories per serving, for a total of 92 calories saved per serving.

Baked French Toast with Raspberry Syrup

For years, my wife made the same baked French toast on Christmas morning that was loaded with heavy cream and brown sugar. We recently came up with this new and improved version, and our guests were floored that it had absolutely no added sugar. The grapefruit provides a subtle sweetness, while the raspberry syrup pushes it over the edge. If you want to make this more exotic, you can add sweet spices to the syrup, such as Chinese five-spice or cardamom.

French Toast Ingredients

One 13- to 16-ounce loaf French bread (preferably day-old)

8 large eggs

2 cups whole milk

1 cup skim milk

1 cup freshly squeezed grapefruit juice

¼ cup agave nectar

1 teaspoon pure vanilla extract

¼ teaspoon ground cinnamon

¼ teaspoon ground nutmeg

¼ teaspoon salt

Canola oil spray

Raspberry Syrup

½ cup freshly squeezed lemon juice

1 teaspoon grated lemon zest

¼ cup agave nectar

½ cup of fresh raspberries

Directions

Cut the bread into 2-inch cubes. In a large bowl, combine the eggs, whole milk, skim milk, grapefruit juice, agave nectar, vanilla, cinnamon, nutmeg, and salt. Add the bread cubes and stir to coat. Spray a 13 by 9-inch baking pan with canola oil and pour in the bread and liquid. Let the bread soak for 3 hours, or as long as overnight, in the refrigerator.

Preheat the oven to 325 degrees F.

Bake until golden brown, about 40 minutes.

Remove the French toast from the oven and let it cool for a few minutes.

While the French toast is cooling, make the raspberry syrup: Mix lemon juice, lemon zest, raspberries, and agave nectar in a saucepan and bring to a boil. Turn down the heat to low and let simmer for 5 minutes. Cut the French toast into 6 portions and serve with the warm raspberry syrup.

When you are ready to eat, let the miracle berry tablet dissolve on your tongue and then enjoy the dish.

Replacing ¼ cup of sugar with the sweetness from the berry saves 32 calories per serving.
Replacing conventional syrup with our Raspberry Syrup saves an additional
60 calories per serving, for a total of 92 calories saved per serving.

Cherry Pop Tarts

I love Pop Tarts, and there really is no better way to have one than with this recipe. The spiced cherry jam provides the necessary acid, which works nicely with the miracle berry.

Ingredients

Flour, for rolling the dough	1 large egg
1 recipe Pop Tart Dough (page 28)	1 tablespoon water
1 cup Spiced Cherry Jam (page 257)	

Directions

Preheat the oven to 350 degrees F. Line a baking sheet with parchment paper.

On a floured surface, roll the dough into a ¼-inch-thick sheet. Cut into twelve 3-inch squares. Place 2 heaping tablespoons of cherry jam on six of the squares. Beat together the egg and water, and brush the edges of each square with the egg wash. Place another square of dough on top. Using a fork, seal and crimp the edges. Transfer the tarts to the baking sheet. Brush the tops with the egg wash. Bake for 15 to 18 minutes, until golden. Allow to cool before serving.

When you are ready to eat, let the miracle berry tablet dissolve on your tongue and then enjoy the dish.

Replacing 26 tablespoons of sugar with 13 tablespoons of agave nectar and the sweetness from the berry saves 79 calories per serving.

Raisin Nut Pop Tarts

MAKES 6 TARTS (6 SERVINGS)

In this recipe, the acidity comes from the raisin nut spread, which the miracle berry makes effectively sweet.

Ingredients

Flour, for rolling the dough

1 recipe Pop Tart Dough (page 28)

1 cup Raisin Nut Spread (page 260)

1 large egg

1 tablespoon water

Directions

Preheat the oven to 350 degrees F. Line a baking sheet with parchment paper.

On a floured surface, roll the dough into a ¼-inch-thick sheet. Cut into twelve 3-inch squares. Place 2 heaping tablespoons of raisin nut spread on six of the squares. Beat together the egg and water, and brush the edges of each square with the egg wash. Place another square of dough on top. Using a fork, seal and crimp the edges. Transfer the tarts to the baking sheet. Brush the tops with egg wash. Bake for 15 to 18 minutes, until golden. Allow to cool before serving.

When you are ready to eat, let the miracle berry tablet dissolve on your tongue and then enjoy the dish.

Replacing 2 tablespoons of sugar and approximately ⅓ cup of brown sugar with 1 tablespoon of agave nectar and the sweetness from the berry saves 64 calories per serving.

Pop Tart Dough

MAKES TWELVE 3-INCH SQUARES (ENOUGH FOR 6 TARTS)

Ingredients

2 cups unbleached all-purpose flour

1 teaspoon salt

½ pound (2 sticks) unsalted butter, frozen and diced

1 tablespoon agave nectar

1 large egg

Directions

In a food processor, combine the flour and salt. Add the butter and pulse until it forms a coarse meal. Add the agave nectar and egg, and pulse until the dough comes together in a ball. Transfer the dough to a large sheet of plastic wrap and pull up the sides to form a disk. Wrap tightly. Refrigerate for at least 30 minutes before rolling.

When you are ready to eat, let the miracle berry tablet dissolve on your tongue and then enjoy the dish.

Replacing 2 tablespoons of sugar with 1 tablespoon of agave nectar and the sweetness from the berry saves 6 calories per serving.

Homemade Donuts

This donut recipe is one of my favorites, and is designed to replace a standard powdered sugar donut. There is no obvious acid in this recipe, but I will explain why it works: This donut has a lightly fermented dough, which, without the miracle berry, would taste sour. With the miracle berry, that sourness tastes sweet. So the natural fermentation provides the sweetness. Even though the recipe calls for the yeast and water to sit for 10 minutes, I recommend playing around with longer times. The longer it sits, the more sour—and the sweeter it tastes with the miracle berry. Love it!

Ingredients

One ¼-ounce package dry active
yeast (2 ¼ teaspoons)

½ cup warm water (100 degrees F)

3 cups unbleached all-purpose flour,
plus more for kneading

½ teaspoon salt

1 large egg, beaten

1 tablespoon unsalted butter, melted

1 teaspoon honey

Canola oil spray

1 quart vegetable oil, for deep-frying

Directions

Dissolve the yeast in the warm water and let sit for 10 minutes until creamy. In a large bowl, mix flour and salt and make a well in the center. Add the egg, butter, honey, and yeast mixture, incorporating the flour from the sides of the bowl until a dough forms. Turn out onto a floured work surface and knead for 7 minutes.

Spray a clean large bowl lightly with canola oil. Place the dough in the bowl. Cover the bowl with a damp cloth and place somewhere warm until the dough has doubled in size, approximately 1 hour.

On a lightly floured surface, roll out the dough so it is about half an inch thick. Cut twelve circles with a 4-inch donut cutter. Remove the donut holes. Let the donuts and holes rise for 10 minutes more.

In a Dutch oven, heat the vegetable oil to 350 degrees F. A few at a time, fry the donuts for 45 seconds, then carefully turn over and cook for another 45 seconds. Fry the donut holes for 30 seconds, then flip and fry for another 30 seconds. Drain on a wire rack.

When you are ready to eat, let the miracle berry tablet dissolve on your tongue and then enjoy the dish.

Replacing ¼ cup of sugar with 1 teaspoon of honey
and the sweetness from the berry saves 16 calories per donut.

Scones

Making pastries from scratch is not complicated. One great trick here is to freeze the butter for 30 minutes to make grating it easier. The tiny bits of cold butter in the dough will create lots of crisp, flaky, delicious layers when they bake. Even though the caloric savings in this recipe only reflect the sugar that is omitted, another caloric benefit comes from using more sour cream and less butter than in a traditional scone recipe. The sour cream also provides additional sweetness here.

Ingredients

2 cups unbleached all-purpose flour, plus more for the work surface

1 teaspoon baking powder

¼ teaspoon baking soda

½ teaspoon salt

8 tablespoons (1 stick) unsalted butter, frozen

½ cup raisins or dried currants (dried cherries or chopped dried apricots also work nicely)

1 large egg

¼ cup honey

½ cup sour cream

2 tablespoons skim milk

Directions

Preheat the oven to 400 degrees F. Line a baking sheet with parchment paper.

In a large bowl, mix the flour, baking powder, baking soda, and salt. Grate the butter into the flour mixture on the largest holes of a box grater. Using your fingers, gently work the butter into the flour until the mixture is crumbly. Stir in the raisins. In a small bowl, beat the egg, honey, and sour cream until smooth. Stir into flour mixture until a sticky dough starts to form. It may seem like the mixture is too dry and needs more liquid, but press the dough together with your hands until it comes together.

Turn out the dough onto a floured surface. Pat into a circle and roll to ¾-inch thick. Cut into eight wedges (like a pizza). Brush with the milk and place 1 inch apart on the baking sheet. Bake for 15 to 17 minutes, or until golden. Let cool before eating.

When you are ready to eat, let the miracle berry tablet dissolve on your tongue and then enjoy the dish.

Replacing ½ cup of sugar with ¼ cup of honey
and the sweetness from the berry saves 16 calories per scone.

Baked Apple Oatmeal

I really enjoy a bowl of oatmeal and brown sugar on a cold morning. With this recipe, oatmeal really tastes better without adding any sugar; this is achieved by using grapefruit juice's acidity to provide a medium level of sweetness. If you like your oatmeal even sweeter, add a tablespoon of lemon juice and that should do the trick.

Ingredients

Canola oil spray

3 ½ cups skim milk

¼ cup honey

2 teaspoons unsalted butter
or margarine

½ teaspoon salt

½ teaspoon ground cinnamon

2 cups old-fashioned rolled oats

2 cups chopped, peeled, and
cored apples (any variety)

1 cup chopped walnuts

1 cup raisins

1 cup wheat germ

½ cup freshly squeezed grapefruit
juice

Directions

Preheat the oven to 350 degrees F. Lightly spray a 2-quart baking dish with canola oil.

In a saucepan, heat the milk, honey, butter, salt, and cinnamon. Add the oats, apples, nuts, raisins, wheat germ, and grapefruit juice. Mix gently. Spoon into the baking dish. Cover and bake for 45 minutes.

When you are ready to eat, let the miracle berry tablet dissolve on your tongue and then enjoy the dish.

Replacing 1 cup of brown sugar with ¼ cup of honey
and the sweetness from the berry saves 96 calories per serving.

Sweet Yogurt Parfait

MAKES 1 SERVING

This is a really simple recipe. One could argue that all of these flavors taste great on their own. But the reality is that flavored yogurt contains 1 teaspoon of sugar per serving. This version is wonderfully sweet from the lemon juice and the natural acidity of the yogurt, and healthier, too. Greek-style yogurt is especially good in this recipe.

Ingredients

1 cup plain nonfat yogurt

½ cup freshly squeezed lemon juice

½ cup strawberries, blueberries, raspberries, or blackberries

¼ cup granola

Directions

Combine the yogurt and lemon juice. In a tall glass, layer half each of the yogurt, berries, and granola. Repeat.

When you are ready to eat, let the miracle berry tablet dissolve on your tongue and then enjoy the dish.

---

*Replacing 3 tablespoons of sugar from the yogurt
with the sweetness from the berry saves 144 calories.*

MUFFINS AND QUICK BREADS

Raspberry Cheesecake Muffins

Raspberries can be really amazing with the miracle berry. If you are only able to purchase slightly unripened raspberries, not to worry. The miracle berry turns their sourness sweet and decadent. The cream cheese lends a wonderful supple texture and adds sweetness as well.

Ingredients

½ cup agave nectar

3 ounces reduced-fat cream cheese, softened

3 large eggs

1 ½ teaspoons pure vanilla extract

6 tablespoons (¾ stick) unsalted butter

2 cups unbleached all-purpose flour

2 ½ teaspoons baking powder

½ teaspoon salt

1 cup fresh raspberries

Directions

Preheat the oven to 400 degrees F. Line a regular muffin pan with paper liners.

In a bowl, beat ¼ cup of the agave nectar, the cream cheese, 1 of the eggs, and ½ teaspoon of the vanilla until completely smooth. Set aside.

In a saucepan, combine the butter and the remaining 1 teaspoon vanilla over medium heat until butter is melted. Cool slightly. Beat in the remaining 2 eggs, one at a time. In a large bowl, combine the flour, baking powder, salt, and the remaining ¼ cup agave nectar. Stir in the butter-egg mixture until combined. Gently fold in the raspberries.

Scoop into the muffin cups, filling each halfway. Spoon approximately 2 teaspoons of the cream cheese mixture on top of each muffin. Bake for about 20 minutes or until the muffins are springy but firm.

Transfer the muffins to a wire rack to cool before serving. The muffins can be stored in an airtight container at room temperature for 2 to 3 days.

When you are ready to eat, let the miracle berry tablet dissolve on your tongue and then enjoy the dish.

———————————

Replacing 1 cup of sugar with ½ cup of agave nectar
and the sweetness from the berry saves 24 calories per serving.

Blueberry Muffins

MAKES 12 MUFFINS (12 SERVINGS)

In this recipe, we add the lime juice for an extra layer of sweetness, and the yogurt complements the blueberries perfectly. These are great as a dessert served with any one of the ice creams in this book.

Ingredients

3 ½ cups cake flour (see note)

1 teaspoon baking soda

2 teaspoons baking powder

Big pinch of salt

1 ½ cups fresh blueberries

½ cup agave nectar

½ cup freshly squeezed lime juice

½ cup vegetable oil

1 large egg

½ cup plain nonfat yogurt

Directions

Preheat the oven to 375 degrees F. Line a regular muffin pan with paper liners.

Sift the flour, baking soda, baking powder, and salt into a large bowl. Mix until combined. Sprinkle 1 tablespoon of the mixture over 1 cup of the blueberries.

In another large bowl, whisk together the agave nectar, lime juice, oil, egg, and yogurt. Add the dry flour mixture and stir just until moistened. Do not overmix. Fold in the floured blueberries and stir only three more times.

Scoop the batter into the muffin cups, filling each only two-thirds full. Top with the remaining ½ cup berries, pressing them down lightly into the batter. Place in the oven and turn up the temperature to 400 degrees F. Bake for 20 to 25 minutes, rotating the pan halfway through. If you can place a knife into the muffin and it comes out clean, they are done. If not, bake for 2 more minutes and test again.

Transfer the muffins to a wire rack to cool before serving. The muffins can be stored in an airtight container at room temperature for 2 to 3 days.

NOTE: If you don't have cake flour, you can make your own. For every cup of cake flour needed, place 2 tablespoons of cornstarch in a 1-cup measure, then fill the rest of the cup with all-purpose flour. Sift the ingredients a few times to aerate the mixture.

When you are ready to eat, let the miracle berry tablet dissolve on your tongue and then enjoy the dish.

Replacing 1 cup plus 1 tablespoon of sugar with ½ cup of agave nectar
and the sweetness from the berry saves 28 calories per serving.

Banana Nut Muffins

My favorite thing about these muffins is the way the buttermilk and lime juice play off each other to produce a subtle sweetness that matches with the bananas perfectly. The bananas add the necessary texture to create an amazing mouthfeel.

Ingredients

Canola oil spray (optional)

8 tablespoons (1 stick) unsalted butter, softened

¼ cup agave nectar

½ cup freshly squeezed lime juice

2 large eggs

2 large ripe bananas, mashed

1 teaspoon pure vanilla extract

2 cups unbleached all-purpose flour

1 teaspoon salt

1 teaspoon baking powder

½ teaspoon baking soda

1 cup low-fat buttermilk (see note)

½ cup chopped pecans

Directions

Preheat the oven to 400 degrees F. Lightly spray a regular muffin pan with canola oil or line with paper liners.

In a large bowl, beat together the butter, agave nectar, and lime juice until combined. Beat in the eggs, one at a time, beating after each addition. Beat in the bananas and vanilla until the mixture is smooth.

In a separate bowl, whisk together the flour, salt, baking powder, and baking soda. Alternate adding the flour mixture and buttermilk to the banana mixture until the dry ingredients are just moistened. Stir in the pecans.

Spoon the batter into the muffin pan, filling the cups two-thirds full. Bake for 20 minutes or until golden brown.

Transfer the muffins to a wire rack to cool before serving. The muffins can be stored in an airtight container at room temperature for 2 to 3 days.

NOTE: To make your own substitute for buttermilk, add 1 tablespoon of cider vinegar or lemon juice to a 1-cup measure. Pour in milk to make 1 cup. Let sit for 5 minutes until curdled like buttermilk.

When you are ready to eat, let the miracle berry tablet dissolve on your tongue and then enjoy the dish.

Replacing ¾ cup of sugar with ¼ cup of agave nectar
and the sweetness from the berry saves 28 calories per serving.

Cinnamon Spice Muffins

MAKES 12 MUFFINS (12 SERVINGS)

Cinnamon is slightly sweet, slightly spicy, and provides a warm, earthy flavor to these muffins. For a more exotic variation, substitute Chinese five-spice powder for the cinnamon. In this recipe, we use ½ cup of freshly squeezed lime juice to boost the sweetness, but lemon juice can be substituted.

Ingredients

5 tablespoons unsalted butter

5 tablespoons vegetable shortening

½ cup agave nectar

2 large eggs

1 cup skim milk

½ cup freshly squeezed lime juice

1 teaspoon salt

3 teaspoons baking powder

1 teaspoon ground cinnamon, plus more for topping

½ teaspoon ground nutmeg

3 cups unbleached all-purpose flour

Directions

Preheat the oven to 350 degrees F. Line a regular muffin pan with paper liners.

With an electric mixer, beat the butter, shortening, and agave nectar until fluffy. Beat in the eggs, milk, lime juice, salt, baking powder, cinnamon, and nutmeg until combined. Stir in the flour until just moistened.

Scoop the batter into the muffin pan, filling the cups two-thirds full. Sprinkle the top of each muffin with ground cinnamon. Bake for about 25 minutes, or until done.

To test for doneness, insert the end of a pairing knife halfway into a muffin and if it comes out clean remove from oven. If the pairing knife is not clean, bake in 5 minute increments until done. Transfer the muffins to a wire rack to cool before serving. The muffins can be stored in an airtight container at room temperature for 2 to 3 days.

When you are ready to eat, let the miracle berry tablet dissolve on your tongue and then enjoy the dish.

Replacing 1 cup of sugar with ½ cup of agave nectar and the sweetness from the berry saves 24 calories per serving.

Cranberry Orange Bread

MAKES ONE 9 BY 5-INCH LOAF (8 SERVINGS)

Cranberries have a natural sourness that plays perfectly with the sweet orange juice in this bread. They are a great match with miracle berries.

Ingredients

8 tablespoons (1 stick) cold unsalted butter, cut into pea-size pieces, plus 1 tablespoon for greasing the pan

2 cups unbleached all-purpose flour, plus more for the pan

1 orange

¾ cup freshly squeezed orange juice

½ teaspoon baking soda

½ teaspoon salt

1 cup agave nectar

1 large egg

1 cup dried, unsweetened cranberries

Directions

Preheat the oven to 350 degrees F. Butter and flour a 9 by 5-inch loaf pan.

Grate the zest from the orange. Slice off the top and bottom. With a paring knife, cut downward from the top to remove the peel and white pith. Cut between the membranes to loosen the sections. Dice the sections into a large bowl. Squeeze any remaining juice from the membranes and add to the diced sections. Add the ¾ cup orange juice.

In another large bowl, combine the flour, baking soda, salt, and orange zest. Cut in the butter with a pastry blender or two forks until the mixture resembles coarse sand. Add the agave nectar, egg, and cranberries to the diced orange sections and juice, and stir to combine. Fold this into the flour mixture, stirring only until moistened. Pour into the loaf pan and bake for 35 to 40 minutes, until a toothpick inserted into the middle comes out clean.

Cool in the pan on a wire rack. The bread can be stored in airtight container at room temperature for 2 to 3 days.

When you are ready to eat, let the miracle berry tablet dissolve on your tongue and then enjoy the dish.

———————————

Replacing 1 ½ cups of sugar with 1 cup of agave nectar
and the sweetness from the berry saves 24 calories per serving.

Apple Spice Bread

MAKES ONE 9 BY 5-INCH LOAF (8 SERVINGS)

The natural acidity in the apples and cider, paired with lime juice, gives this velvet-textured bread just the right amount of sweetness. Dried cherries and almonds would also be a delicious combination in place of the raisins and walnuts.

Ingredients

- 4 tablespoons (½ stick) unsalted butter, plus more for greasing the pan
- 1 ¾ cups unbleached all-purpose flour, plus more for the pan
- 2 Granny Smith apples
- ½ cup freshly squeezed lemon juice
- 1 cup apple cider
- 1 teaspoon ground cinnamon

- ½ teaspoon ground nutmeg
- 1 teaspoon baking soda
- Pinch of kosher salt
- 1 ¼ cups agave nectar
- 1 large egg, beaten
- 1 teaspoon pure vanilla extract
- ½ cup toasted and chopped walnuts
- ½ cup golden raisins

Directions

Preheat the oven to 350 degrees F. Butter and flour a 9 by 5-inch loaf pan.

Peel, core, and dice the apples into ½-inch pieces. In a large skillet, melt the butter over medium heat. Add the apples, lemon juice, and cider. Cook until the apples have softened and the liquid has reduced by half, about 15 minutes. Drain and reserve the apples.

In a large mixing bowl, combine the flour, cinnamon, nutmeg, baking soda, and salt. Make a well in the center and pour in the agave nectar, egg, and vanilla. Stir to combine. Add the apples, walnuts, and raisins. Pour the batter into the loaf pan and bake for 1 hour, or until a toothpick comes out clean.

Let cool in the pan for 10 minutes. Invert onto a wire rack to cool completely.

The bread can be stored in an airtight container at room temperature for 2 to 3 days.

When you are ready to eat, let the miracle berry tablet dissolve on your tongue and then enjoy the dish.

Replacing 2 cups of sugar with 1¼ cup of agave nectar
and the sweetness from the berry saves 42 calories per serving.

STARTERS

Cheese Puffs

MAKES 12 PUFFS (6 SERVINGS)

My wife, Katie, loves to whip up something without a recipe from whatever we have in the fridge. While not every one of her "kitchen improvs" is a hit, this one is. Sometimes she adds minced jalapeño or chipotle pepper, which adds some heat to contrast with the sweetness from the fruit.

Ingredients

8 ounces feta cheese

1 large egg, separated

1 cup chopped dried apricots

½ cup dried cherries

2 tablespoons whole milk (optional)

Salt and ground black pepper

Flour, for the work surface

1 sheet frozen puff pastry, thawed overnight in the refrigerator

Directions

Preheat the oven to 350 degrees F. Line a baking sheet with parchment paper.

In a food processor, blend the feta, egg yolk, apricots, and cherries. The mixture should be pliable but not wet; if it is too thick, add 1 tablespoon of whole milk at a time with the processor running until desired consistency is reached. Season with salt and pepper.

On a floured surface, roll out the puff pastry dough to ⅛-inch thick. Cut in half lengthwise to make two long strips. On one strip, lay 12 spoonfuls of cheese mixture, evenly spaced. Lightly beat the egg white. Brush the egg white on the remaining strip of dough and carefully lay it on top of the other, enclosing the mounds of cheese like ravioli. Using your fingers, gently press around each mound and cut the "ravioli" into squares. Place on the baking sheet, brush with egg white, and bake for 20 minutes or until golden brown and serve immediately.

When you are ready to eat, let the miracle berry tablet dissolve on your tongue and then enjoy the dish.

Replacing ¼ cup of sugar with the sweetness from the berry saves 32 calories per serving.

Brie en Croûte

With this recipe, the red wine will wind up tasting like port, but without all the additional sugar that's in port. The average wheel of supermarket brie will taste like something right out of the Camembert region of France, the stuff that's cave ripened, that you could eat with a spoon. Mmmm.

Ingredients

½ cup walnuts

½ tablespoon honey

½ teaspoon salt

2 tablespoons red wine

¼ cup raisins

Flour, for rolling the pastry

1 sheet frozen puff pastry, thawed overnight in the refrigerator

One 6- to 8-ounce round brie cheese

1 large egg

1 tablespoon water

1 tablespoon finely chopped fresh rosemary

Directions

Preheat the oven to 300 degrees F. Line two baking sheets with parchment paper.

Combine the walnuts, honey, and salt and spread on one baking sheet. Roast for 15 minutes. Remove from oven and turn up the oven temperature to 400 degrees F.

In a small saucepan, heat the wine until warm. Stir in the raisins and turn off the heat. Let sit for about 10 minutes until the raisins have plumped up and absorbed the wine. The raisins will not absorb all of the wine; there will be about a tablespoon left over.

On a floured surface, gently roll out the puff pastry to form a 14-inch square. Transfer to the second baking sheet. Place the brie in the center of the pastry and top with the walnuts and raisins. Pull the pastry up over the sides of the brie, gathering it at the top into a neat bundle. Gently squeeze together the excess dough. Beat the egg and water and brush the egg wash over the top and sides of the pastry.

Bake for 20 to 25 minutes, until pastry is golden brown. Let sit for 15 to 20 minutes before slicing. Garnish with the rosemary.

When you are ready to eat, let the miracle berry tablet dissolve on your tongue and then enjoy the dish.

Replacing ¼ cup of sugar (in the port) with the sweetness from the berry saves 27 to 40 calories per serving.

Spicy Apricot Chicken Wings

MAKES 6 SERVINGS (APPROXIMATELY 3 WINGS PER SERVING)

My favorite chicken wing place is a Korean strip mall take-out restaurant in Chicago. You walk in and an eighty-year-old woman cooks your wings from start to finish, which takes about an hour. Decades of expertise go into a little chicken wing that is complete perfection. That was the standard for creating this recipe.

Don't be afraid to double the cayenne pepper in this recipe. If you can take the heat, bump it up. They're sweet, spicy, and addictive.

Ingredients

1 cup dried apricots, chopped

½ cup freshly squeezed lime juice

1 clove garlic, smashed

1 cup water

½ teaspoon ground black pepper

2 ¼ teaspoons salt

½ teaspoon ground cumin

½ teaspoon cayenne pepper

2 pounds whole chicken wings

Directions

In a blender or food processor, puree the apricots, lime juice, garlic, water, black pepper, salt, cumin, and cayenne until smooth. If the mixture is too chunky, add more water until smooth. Pour half into a large bowl and reserve the other half for a dipping sauce. Add the wings to the marinade, cover, and refrigerate for at least 4 hours or overnight.

Preheat the oven to 350 degrees F. Line a baking sheet with parchment paper.

Remove the wings from the marinade and spread on the baking sheet. Bake for 30 minutes or until wings are browned and crispy. Serve with the reserved dipping sauce.

When you are ready to eat, let the miracle berry tablet dissolve on your tongue and then enjoy the dish.

Replacing ½ cup of sugar with the sweetness from the berry saves 64 calories per serving.

Pork Curry Dumplings with Sweet Ginger Garlic Sauce

MAKES 24 DUMPLINGS (6 SERVINGS)

The miracle berries accentuate the earthiness of the curry without all the heat in these flavorful dumplings. Rice vinegar and lime juice play well off each other to provide a bright and complex accompaniment to the dumplings.

Ingredients

1 pound ground pork

½ large yellow onion, minced

½ cup cilantro, minced

½ teaspoon crushed red pepper flakes

2 teaspoons red curry paste

½ teaspoon chili powder

¼ teaspoon onion powder

¼ teaspoon garlic powder

1 tablespoon agave nectar

24 wonton or gyoza wrappers

Sweet Ginger Garlic Sauce (recipe follows), for serving

Directions

In a large bowl, combine everything except the wonton wrappers and sauce until thoroughly mixed. Using your hands works best.

Working in batches, lay the wonton wrappers on a flat surface and place a heaping spoonful of the filling in the center of each wrapper. Moisten the edges with water and bring the edges together at the top so they meet. Press to seal while making small folds about ¼ inch apart. Cover with damp paper towel while forming the remaining dumplings.

Bring a large pot of water to a boil. Turn down the heat to a simmer, gently lower the dumplings into the water and cook until the dumplings have been translucent and floating for about 3 minutes, about 5 minutes total. Carefully remove with a slotted spoon and, using a paper towel, blot the dumplings to remove excess water. Serve hot with dipping sauce.

Sweet Ginger Garlic Sauce
MAKES ABOUT 1 CUP

Ingredients

¼ cup reduced-sodium soy sauce

¼ cup honey

¼ cup rice vinegar

1 clove garlic, minced

1 tablespoon grated fresh ginger

2 tablespoons freshly squeezed lime juice

2 teaspoons cornstarch

Directions

Combine the soy sauce, honey, vinegar, garlic, and ginger in a small saucepan. Bring to a boil. Make a slurry with the lime juice and cornstarch, add to the sauce, and stir until thickened.

When you are ready to eat, let the miracle berry tablet dissolve on your tongue and then enjoy the dish.

Replacing ½ cup of brown sugar with ¼ cup of honey, 1 tablespoon of agave nectar, and the sweetness from the berry saves 17 calories per serving.

Shrimp Pot Stickers

MAKES 24 POT STICKERS (6 SERVINGS)

There is something so satisfying about the combination of textures in a well-made pot sticker—crispy edges and soft, supple top, plus the surprise of sweet and spicy sauce that make these everyone's favorite appetizer. Here we are eliminating sugar in both the pot sticker and dipping sauce by adding lemon juice, which is a natural friend to shrimp. I prefer to pan-fry these pot stickers, but you can also steam them.

Ingredients

- 1 pound of shrimp, peeled and deveined
- 1 tablespoon freshly squeezed lemon juice
- 1 scallion (green onion), sliced into very thin rings
- 2 tablespoons reduced-sodium soy sauce
- 1 tablespoon grated fresh ginger
- 1 teaspoon cayenne pepper
- 2 cloves garlic, sliced
- 1 tablespoon chopped fresh cilantro
- 1 teaspoon salt
- 24 wonton or gyoza wrappers
- 1 tablespoon toasted sesame oil
- Soy Dipping Sauce (recipe follows), for serving

Directions

Pat shrimp dry with paper towels. Chop shrimp into ¼-inch pieces. In a food processor, mix shrimp, lemon juice, scallion, soy sauce, ginger, cayenne, garlic, cilantro, and salt and pulse until the mixture is well blended.

Working in batches, lay the wonton wrappers on a flat surface and place a heaping spoonful of filling in the center of each wrapper. Moisten the edges with water and bring the edges together at the top so they meet and seal completely shut. Press to seal while making small folds about ¼ inch apart. Cover with a damp paper towel while forming the remaining dumplings.

Heat the sesame oil in a large skillet over medium heat. Carefully lay pot stickers in the pan in one layer, being careful not to crowd the pan. Sear for 2 minutes, then pour ¼ cup of water into the pan, turn down the heat to low, and cover. Cook for 3 to 5 minutes, until the wonton wrappers are tender and filling is cooked through. Place cooked dumplings on a plate and cover with plastic wrap to keep hot. Repeat in batches, adding additional oil to pan as needed. Serve when all dumplings are cooked.

Soy Dipping Sauce
MAKES ABOUT 10 TABLESPOONS SAUCE (6 SERVINGS)

Ingredients

1 cup reduced-sodium soy sauce   2 teaspoons wasabi paste
½ cup freshly squeezed lime juice   2 teaspoons kosher salt

Directions

Whisk together all the ingredients.

When you are ready to eat, let the miracle berry tablet dissolve on your tongue and then enjoy the dish.

Replacing ½ cup of sugar with the sweetness from the berry saves 64 calories per serving.

Crab Rangoon
with Orange Dipping Sauce

MAKES 24 DUMPLINGS (6 SERVINGS)

It took me a long time to master a perfect regular crab Rangoon, so adapting the recipe for miracle berries was much more fun. The orange juice works with the red pepper flakes to complement the crab nicely.

Ingredients

8 ounces reduced-fat cream cheese, softened

½ pound fresh crabmeat, drained and flaked

2 tablespoons chopped drained water chestnuts

Kernels cut from 2 ears fresh corn (about 1 cup)

2 tablespoons chopped fresh cilantro

½ teaspoon garlic powder

¼ teaspoon paprika

¼ teaspoon cayenne pepper

24 wonton wrappers

1 large egg

1 tablespoon water

1 quart peanut or canola oil, for deep-frying

Orange Dipping Sauce (recipe follows), for serving

Directions

Combine the cream cheese, crab, water chestnuts, corn, cilantro, garlic powder, paprika, and cayenne.

Working in batches, lay the wonton wrappers on a flat surface. Beat the egg and water and brush the edges of a wonton wrapper with the egg wash. Place a heaping spoonful of filling in the center. Fold the wrapper in half diagonally to form a triangle, pressing the edges to seal. Moisten one of the bottom corners with water. Create a crown by pulling the two bottom corners together, pressing to seal. Cover with a damp paper towel while forming the remaining dumplings.

Heat the oil in a large, heavy saucepan to 350 degrees F. Fry the dumplings in 3 batches until golden brown. Drain on paper towels. Hold first batch in a 250-degree oven until remaining batches are complete. Serve with orange dipping sauce.

Orange Dipping Sauce
MAKES 1 CUP

Ingredients

1 cup freshly squeezed orange juice

1 teaspoon cornstarch

¼ teaspoon crushed red pepper flakes

1 teaspoon garlic, minced

1 teaspoon honey

Directions

In a small saucepan, combine all the ingredients and bring to a boil. Turn down the heat to a simmer and cook until the sauce thickens. Turn off the heat and let cool before serving.

When you are ready to eat, let the miracle berry tablet dissolve on your tongue and then enjoy the dish.

Replacing ½ cup of sugar from the dipping sauce and the dumpling filling
with 1 teaspoon of honey and the sweetness from the berry saves 61 calories per serving.

Sweet and Spicy Beef and Manchego Empanadas

MAKES 24 EMPANADAS (12 SERVINGS)

In Portland, Oregon, I cooked twenty different tapas dishes a night as sous chef at a Spanish restaurant. The beef and Manchego empanada was the very best. The chef's mother, Mercedes, who was from the Rioja region of Spain, taught me how to make them. I tried to get this recipe as close to hers as possible, testing it with Chris Jones until we were happy with the authentic flavor. The apple cider in the filling blends well with the Manchego and the miracle berries. It adds the slightly sweet character that is balanced perfectly with the spices.

In a pinch, you can use premade empanada dough circles, but it's well worth the time to make your own, which is sweet and tender and soaks up the savory filling beautifully.

Ingredients

¼ large yellow onion, minced

1 clove garlic, minced

1 teaspoon olive oil, plus more
   for the baking sheet

1 pound ground beef

2 tablespoons raisins

½ cup apple cider

1 teaspoon salt

2 teaspoons cayenne pepper

2 tablespoons paprika

1 tablespoon ground cumin

12 ounces Manchego cheese,
   shredded (about 3 cups)

1 recipe Empanada Dough
   (recipe follows) or 24 store-bought
   empanada circles

1 egg

1 tablespoon water

Directions

In a large skillet over medium-high heat, sauté the onion and garlic in the oil until softened, about 3 minutes. Add the ground beef and cook until browned, stirring frequently to break up clumps. Add the raisins, cider, salt, cayenne, paprika, and cumin. Drain off any excess fat. Turn off the heat and stir in the cheese. Check for seasoning and add more salt and cayenne if necessary.

Preheat the oven to 400 degrees F. Lightly grease a baking sheet with olive oil. If using homemade empanada dough, flour the work surface lightly. Roll out the empanada dough to ⅛-inch thickness and cut out 24 circles with a 3-inch-diameter cutter.

Working in batches, top each circle with a heaping spoonful of filling. Wet the edges of the dough with water and fold into a half-circle. Crimp the edges with a fork to seal. Place on the baking sheet. Beat the egg with the water and brush the empanadas with the egg wash. Bake for 15 minutes or until golden, cool before serving.

You can freeze uncooked empanadas for up to a month.

Empanada Dough
MAKES ENOUGH FOR 24 EMPANADAS

Ingredients

4 cups unbleached all-purpose
   flour

1 teaspoon salt

2 tablespoons cold butter,
   cut into ½-inch cubes

12 tablespoons vegetable shortening,
   chilled

2 large egg yolks

¾ cup ice water

2 tablespoons honey

Directions

Sift the flour into a large bowl. Stir in the salt. Cut the butter and shortening into the flour with a pastry blender or fork, or crumble with your fingers, until the butter and shortening pieces are about the size of peas. The colder the butter and shortening are to start, the better the final texture will be.

Whisk the egg yolks with the ice water and honey. Pour half into the dry ingredients and stir until the dough starts to come together. Knead the dough in the bowl, gradually adding more of the liquid a little at a time until the dough is smooth. You may need to add a bit more water, but don't add too much. The dough should be a little "shaggy" until it's had time to rest in the refrigerator. Cover with plastic wrap and chill for 1 hour (or as long as 2 days). The dough should be soft and smooth, and not elastic—if you poke it with your finger, the indentation should remain.

After the dough has rested in the refrigerator, divide it into 24 portions.

This recipe is for baked empanadas. If you plan to fry your empanadas, omit the egg yolks and roll the dough out slightly thinner, less than ¼-inch thick.

When you are ready to eat, let the miracle berry tablet dissolve on your tongue and then enjoy the dish.

―――――――――――

Replacing 1 ½ cups of sugar from the empanada dough and with 2 tablespoons of honey and the sweetness from the berry saves 86 calories per serving.

Butternut Squash Soup

MAKES 8 SERVINGS

In this soup, we add sour cream for richness and sweetness. Very seldom does this miracle berry trick work in savory dishes, because the sour cream will usually translate into an almost cheesecake-like flavor. However, here that flavor plays well with the sweetness of the butternut squash and the heat of the ginger and jalapeño.

Ingredients

2 tablespoons unsalted butter

1 yellow onion, diced

2 teaspoons grated fresh ginger

1 jalapeño pepper, seeded and diced

2 pounds butternut squash, peeled, seeded, and cubed

1 ¾ cups low-sodium chicken broth

One 12-ounce can evaporated milk

½ cup coconut milk

1 tablespoon agave nectar

Salt and ground black pepper

1 cup lemon juice

1 tablespoon chopped fresh sage, or to taste

1 cup sour cream

Directions

Melt the butter in a large pot over medium heat. Stir in the onion, ginger, and jalapeño pepper. Cook and stir until the onion has softened and is translucent, about 7 minutes. Add the butternut squash and chicken broth and turn up the heat to high. When the soup comes to a boil, turn down the heat to medium-low, cover, and simmer until the squash is tender, about 30 minutes.

Stir in the evaporated milk, coconut milk, agave nectar, and salt and pepper to taste. Cook for 5 minutes more, stirring occasionally. Add lemon juice and puree in the pot with an immersion blender, or in batches in a blender. Make sure not to fill the blender more than halfway and to cover tightly with the lid and a kitchen towel before blending. Garnish with sour cream and sage.

When you are ready to eat, let the miracle berry tablet dissolve on your tongue and then enjoy the dish.

---

*Replacing ⅓ cup of sugar with 1 tablespoon of agave nectar
and the sweetness from the berry saves 25 calories per serving.*

MAINS AND SIDES

Sweet Chili Shrimp

MAKES 4 SERVINGS

These are a modified version of firecracker shrimp, without all the sugar. Miracle berries make shrimp (and all shellfish) sweeter and just plain better.

Ingredients

2 tablespoons honey

⅔ cup rice vinegar or white wine vinegar

4 large cloves garlic, minced

¾ teaspoon crushed red pepper flakes

¾ teaspoon salt

½ cup water

½ cup plus 2 teaspoons cornstarch

1 pound raw shrimp, peeled and deveined

Canola or peanut oil, for frying

½ cup unbleached all-purpose flour

Directions

Combine the honey, vinegar, garlic, red pepper flakes, and salt in a saucepan and bring to a boil. In a small bowl, mix the water and 2 teaspoons of the cornstarch until smooth. Slowly stir the cornstarch mixture into the hot liquid, turn off the heat and stir until thickened. Reserve half of the sauce for dipping. Pour the remaining half over the shrimp. Toss to coat. Marinate for 30 minutes or as long as overnight. (Refrigerate if marinating more than 30 minutes.)

In a large skillet, heat 1 inch of oil to 275 degrees F. Combine the flour and the remaining ½ cup cornstarch. Working in batches if necessary, remove the shrimp from the marinade, dredge in the flour mixture, and immediately drop into the hot oil. Fry for 2 minutes, or until golden brown. Do not flour the shrimp ahead of time, or the coating will get gummy. Remove with a slotted spoon and drain on a wire rack. Serve hot with the reserved marinade.

When you are ready to eat, let the miracle berry tablet dissolve on your tongue and then enjoy the dish.

———————————

Replacing ½ cup of sugar with 2 tablespoons of honey
and the sweetness from the berry saves 64 calories per serving.

Pad Thai

Typically pad thai has sugar added to it. What makes this recipe special is not only that we are removing the sugar, but we are also enhancing the other flavors in the dish with the miracle berry. The hot pepper sauce really takes on another, fruitier dimension of flavor, while harmonizing perfectly with the shrimp.

Diced chicken or sautéed firm tofu make great substitutes for the shrimp.

Ingredients

8 ounces rice vermicelli noodles
Boiling water
3 tablespoons vegetable oil
¼ pound ground chicken or turkey
1 teaspoon hot pepper sauce
1 red bell pepper, thinly sliced
½ pound raw shrimp, peeled and deveined
3 cloves garlic, minced
2 teaspoons grated fresh ginger

½ cup vegetable or low-sodium chicken broth
½ cup fire-roasted red peppers, drained and pureed
¼ cup freshly squeezed lime juice
1 tablespoon agave nectar
3 tablespoons fish sauce
1 ½ cups bean sprouts
3 scallions (green onions), thinly sliced
¼ cup chopped fresh cilantro
¼ cup chopped peanuts

Directions

Cover the noodles with boiling water and let stand for 5 minutes; drain and reserve.

Heat half the oil in a wok or deep skillet over high heat. Crumble in the chicken and add the hot sauce. Stir-fry for 3 to 5 minutes, until browned. Transfer to a platter.

Heat the remaining oil and add the sliced pepper to the pan. Stir-fry for 3 minutes. Add the shrimp and stir-fry for another minute. Stir in garlic, ginger, broth, red pepper puree, lime juice, agave nectar, and fish sauce. Bring to a boil. Add the noodles and chicken; toss to combine. Heat through.

Remove from the heat. Add the bean sprouts and toss gently. Sprinkle with the scallions, cilantro, and peanuts. Serve immediately.

When you are ready to eat, let the miracle berry tablet dissolve on your tongue and then enjoy the dish.

-----

*Replacing ½ cup of sugar with 1 tablespoon of agave nectar
and the sweetness from the berry saves 81 calories per serving.*

Pulled Pork Sandwiches

This is a wonderfully complex recipe, with many layers of flavors working together. All of my favorite elements with the miracle berry are present here—it utilizes pineapple and cider vinegar for acidity and depth, plus adds a fruity dimension to the chili powder. Combined, it all makes for a one-of-a-kind experience.

I know that it's blasphemous to suggest pulled pork from a slow cooker, but sometimes you just need a "set it and forget it" recipe that is tasty and great for a crowd. While I love making a day of smoking my own meats, low and slow, this recipe is a real keeper, too. Marinate the meat the night before you want to serve it, and pop it into the slow cooker in the morning. That's it!

Ingredients

- 3 pounds pork shoulder in one piece
- 2 quarts apple cider vinegar, or more as needed
- 1 quart water, or more as needed
- ¼ cup kosher salt
- 1 large yellow onion, cut into 8 wedges
- ¼ cup honey
- ¼ cup tamarind paste
- ¼ cup pineapple juice
- 1 tablespoon ground cumin
- 1 tablespoon chili powder
- 1 tablespoon ground mustard
- 8 soft sandwich rolls, split
- 1 recipe Southwestern Coleslaw (page 107), for serving

Directions

Place the pork shoulder in the ceramic liner of a slow cooker. Pour enough apple cider vinegar and water to completely cover the pork, maintaining a 2-to-1 ratio of vinegar to water. Add the salt. Cover and put the liner in the refrigerator. Marinate the pork for 12 to 24 hours.

Drain enough of the liquid from the liner until about ½ inch of the pork is left exposed. Add the onion, honey, tamarind, and pineapple juice to the remaining liquid. Stir in the cumin, chili powder, and mustard. Place the liner into the slow cooker, cover, and cook on high until the pork is tender and falls apart easily, 8 to 10 hours.

Carefully remove pork from liquid, transfer to a cutting board, and shred the meat using two forks. Discard any excess fat. Serve on soft rolls with coleslaw.

When you are ready to eat, let the miracle berry tablet dissolve on your tongue and then enjoy the dish.

---

*Replacing 2 cups of packed brown sugar with ¼ cup of honey
and the sweetness from the berry saves 176 calories per serving.
In the slaw, replacing ½ cup of sugar with the sweetness from the berry
saves an additional 48 calories per serving, for a total of 224 calories saved per serving.*

Rosemary Chicken with Corn Bread Stuffing

MAKES 4 SERVINGS

Classic roast chicken is a great family meal, but sometimes it needs a pick-me-up. The combination of sweet corn bread, salty bacon, and clean, slightly pine-scented rosemary take an ordinary roast chicken to a new level. You only need half of the corn bread for the stuffing, so try making croutons with the rest—they are great on a green salad or crumbled into chili.

Corn Bread

Canola oil spray

1 cup masa harina (corn flour)

1 cup yellow medium-ground cornmeal

¼ cup nonfat dry milk powder

1 teaspoon baking soda

1 tablespoon salt

4 tablespoons (½ stick) unsalted butter, melted

1 cup buttermilk (see note)

3 eggs, lightly beaten

⅓ cup honey

Stuffing

6 slices bacon, cut into ½-inch pieces

½ yellow onion, diced

2 cloves garlic, minced

1 tablespoon thinly sliced fresh sage leaves

1 cup low-sodium chicken broth, plus more as needed

½ cup freshly squeezed lemon juice

One 4- to 5-pound whole roaster chicken, neck and giblets removed

Salt and ground black pepper

5 sprigs fresh rosemary

4 tablespoons (½ stick) unsalted butter, softened

Directions

TO MAKE THE CORN BREAD: Position a rack in the middle of the oven and preheat the oven to 400 degrees F. Spray a 9-inch square baking pan with canola oil. In a large bowl, combine the masa harina, cornmeal, milk powder, baking soda, and salt. Add the butter and mix with a fork or your fingers until the mixture become crumbly. Make a well in the mixture and add the buttermilk, eggs, and honey. Stir until just combined, but do not overmix. Pour into the pan and bake for 20 to 25 minutes or until golden. (Since there is no sugar in the batter, you'll need to bake a little longer to get the caramelization of a good corn bread.) Remove from the oven but leave the oven on at 400 degrees F. Cool the corn bread in the pan on a wire rack.

TO MAKE THE STUFFING: In a large skillet over medium-high heat, cook the bacon until the edges start to get crisp. Add the onion, garlic, and sage and cook until the onion is translucent, about 3 minutes. Add 1 cup chicken broth to the pan, scraping up any browned bits from the bottom of the pan, and cook another minute. Turn off the heat. Crumble half of the corn bread (you should have about 3 cups) and add. (Reserve the remaining corn bread for another use.) Stir the stuffing gently, gradually adding more chicken broth if needed to moisten it slightly. Add the lemon juice.

TO ROAST THE CHICKEN: Pat the chicken dry with paper towels and season the inside generously with salt and pepper. Stuff the chicken with corn bread mixture and tie the legs together with kitchen string to keep the stuffing inside. Season the outside of the chicken with salt and pepper. Lay the rosemary sprigs on bottom of roasting pan. Place chicken on top of the rosemary, breast side up. Using your fingers, gently loosen the skin and spread the butter under the skin. Roast for 30 minutes.

Turn down the oven temperature to 275 degrees F and roast for another hour or until the internal temperature registers 165 degrees F on an instant-read thermometer in the thickest part of the bird. Let rest for 15 minutes before carving.

NOTE: To make your own substitute for buttermilk, pour 1 tablespoon vinegar or lemon juice into a 1-cup measure. Add milk to make 1 cup. Let sit for 5 minutes until curdled like buttermilk.

When you are ready to eat, let the miracle berry tablet dissolve on your tongue and then enjoy the dish.

Replacing 1 cup of sugar and ¼ cup of packed brown sugar with ⅓ cup of honey and the sweetness from the berry saves 159 calories per serving.

Roast Chicken with 30-Minute Mole

MAKES 4 SERVINGS

Some dishes are the perfect match with the miracle berry. Mole is one of them. Not only did all of the Moto chefs prefer this version to the original recipe, but we were able to cut a whopping 776 calories by using cocoa powder instead of Mexican chocolate and using the natural acidity of the tomatoes.

Most people are afraid to make a homemade mole sauce, but this one takes just thirty minutes and has all the depth and complexity of a sauce that cooked all day. My favorite way to eat this is wrapped in a warm flour tortilla, but my daughters prefer it over rice.

Ingredients

2 tablespoons salt

1 tablespoon ground black pepper

1 tablespoon chili powder or ground chile de arbol

1 tablespoon ground cumin

1 tablespoon garlic powder

2 tablespoons unsweetened Dutch-process cocoa powder

1 roaster chicken (5 pounds)

8 tablespoons (1 stick) unsalted butter, softened

4 sprigs fresh cilantro, chopped

30-Minute Mole (recipe follows)

Directions

Preheat the oven to 350 degrees F.

Mix the salt, pepper, chili powder, cumin, garlic powder, and cocoa. Rub on all sides of chicken and inside the cavity. Mix the butter and cilantro. Using your fingers, gently loosen the skin over the breast, thighs, and legs. Spread the butter under the skin on the breast, thigh, and leg meat. Place the chicken breast side up on a rack in a roasting pan. Roast the chicken for 20 minutes.

Turn down the oven temperature to 300 degrees F. Roast for another hour or until the internal temperature registers 165 degrees F on an instant-read thermometer in the thickest part of the bird. Let rest for 15 minutes before carving.

Carve chicken and drizzle generously with mole sauce.

30-Minute Mole
MAKES APPROXIMATELY 2 ½ CUPS

Ingredients

2 tablespoons olive oil

1 yellow onion, sliced

2 jalapeños, seeded and sliced

3 cloves garlic, minced

2 tablespoons salt

2 teaspoons chili powder
   or ground chile de arbol

1 teaspoon ground cumin

1 teaspoon ground black pepper

2 teaspoons unsweetened
   Dutch-process cocoa powder

One 14-ounce can whole peeled
   tomatoes

One 4-ounce can chopped green chiles

Juice of 1 lime

4 sprigs cilantro, coarsely chopped

8 corn tortillas, torn into pieces

Directions

Heat the oil in a large skillet over medium heat. Cook the onion and jalapeños until softened, about 2 minutes. Stir in the garlic, salt, chili powder, cumin, black pepper, and cocoa and cook for another minute. Add the tomatoes, green chiles, and tortillas and cook for 25 minutes, stirring occasionally to prevent the sauce from burning on the bottom of the pan. Puree with an immersion blender in the pan or in a food processor and season with the salt and lime juice. If the mole is too thick, add a little water until it reaches the desired consistency.

When you are ready to eat, let the miracle berry tablet dissolve on your tongue and then enjoy the dish.

———————

Replacing 1 ½ cups of Mexican chocolate from the mole
with the sweetness from the berry saves 133 calories per serving.

Marsala-Less Chicken Marsala with Parmesan Pasta

SERVES 4

Family dinner on Sunday is a big deal in our house. My wife and I have always fed our kids what we're eating, even though they'd probably prefer pasta every night. Our rule is that you have to try everything, even if it's just one bite. They usually end up liking and eating almost everything. My older daughter, Ella, loves anchovies, arugula, kale, and most of all, mushrooms. This dish is very family-friendly—kids get their pasta, but everyone gets to enjoy a tasty, complex dish.

Ingredients

4 boneless, skinless chicken breast halves

Salt and ground black pepper

3 tablespoons olive oil, plus more as needed

2 cups sliced cremini mushrooms

½ onion, sliced

4 cloves garlic, sliced

1 ½ cups low-sodium chicken broth

⅓ cup raisins

2 tablespoons dry sherry vinegar

8 ounces dried fettuccine pasta

1 tablespoon unsalted butter

½ cup grated parmesan cheese (preferably Parmigiano-Reggiano)

Directions

Preheat the oven to 300 degrees F. Season the chicken with salt and pepper and let rest for 20 minutes.

In a large skillet, heat 1 tablespoon of the olive oil over high heat. Cook the chicken for 3 minutes or until nicely browned, turn, and cook another 3 minutes. Transfer to a platter.

If the pan looks dry, add another tablespoon of oil. Over medium-high heat, sauté the mushrooms until browned. Add the onion and garlic. Cook another 2 to 3 minutes, stirring. Add chicken broth, raisins, and vinegar and scrape up any browned bits on the bottom of the pan. Turn down the heat to a simmer and cook for 15 minutes. Blend with immersion blender in the pan or in batches in a blender (being careful not to fill the blender more than halfway in the process). Pour the sauce back into the pan, add the chicken and any collected juices, and cook over medium heat for 10 minutes or until chicken is cooked through.

While chicken is cooking, bring a large pot of water to a boil. Add 1 tablespoon salt. Bring back to a boil and add the pasta. Stir and cook until just al dente. Drain, reserving 1 cup of the pasta water. Toss the pasta in a serving bowl with the remaining 2 tablespoons olive oil, the butter, cheese, 1 teaspoon ground black pepper, and a couple tablespoons of the pasta water, stirring to coat the pasta. Serve with the chicken and the sauce.

When you are ready to eat, let the miracle berry tablet dissolve on your tongue and then enjoy the dish.

Replacing 1 cup of Marsala wine and ½ cup of sherry
with the sweetness from the berry saves 74 calories per serving.

Chicken Kabobs with Tamarind-Date Glaze

MAKES 4 SERVINGS

Tamarind is a sweet-and-sour fruit popular in many Middle Eastern and Mexican foods. Typically molasses is required to balance out the sourness on the pods, but the miracle berry balances this perfectly. You can find the concentrated pulp in Middle Eastern or Asian markets. Serve these kabobs with plenty of warm pita bread.

Tamarind-Date Glaze

1 cup pitted dates, chopped (5 ounces)	Pinch of cayenne pepper
1 ½ cups water	1 tablespoon salt
2 tablespoons tamarind concentrate	¼ cup freshly squeezed lemon juice

Chicken Kabobs

1 cucumber, peeled	Olive oil
4 boneless, skinless chicken breast halves, cut into 1-inch pieces	Salt and ground black pepper
2 yellow onions, thinly sliced	Grated zest of 1 lemon

Directions

TO MAKE THE GLAZE: In a small saucepan, combine the dates, water, honey, tamarind concentrate and cayenne. Simmer for 5 minutes. Transfer the mixture to a food processor and puree until smooth. Set aside half for basting the chicken and half for serving. The glaze can be made ahead and refrigerated for a few days.

TO MAKE THE KABOBS: If using wooden skewers, soak in water for at least 30 minutes. Heat a grill to medium-high or heat a grill pan over medium-high heat. Cut the cucumber in half lengthwise and scoop out seeds with a small spoon. Cut into 1-inch pieces. Brush the chicken, cucumber, and onion slices with oil and sprinkle with salt, pepper, and the lemon zest. Thread the chicken, onion, and cucumber onto skewers. Grill the skewers for 2 minutes. Turn, brush the chicken with the glaze, and grill for 3 minutes more. Turn once more, brush with the glaze, and cook for another 1 to 2 minutes, until chicken is cooked through and the juices run clear when the chicken is poked with fork. Serve with the reserved glaze.

When you are ready to eat, let the miracle berry tablet dissolve on your tongue and then enjoy the dish.

Replacing ½ cup of molasses with the sweetness from the berry saves 116 calories per serving.

Sesame Chicken

MAKES 4 SERVINGS

Shichimi togarashi is a delicious Japanese seven-spice blend that usually contains crushed red pepper flakes, dried orange peel, sesame seeds, nori powder, and ginger, depending on the brand. You can find it at Whole Foods or online. It's delicious on almost anything, but if you are unable to find it, you can substitute a pinch of cayenne pepper or chili powder. In this recipe the cider vinegar is used to flavor and sweeten the chicken, and the miracle berries accentuate the nutty flavor of the sesame.

Ingredients

2 tablespoons minced fresh ginger

4 cloves garlic, minced

1 jalapeño pepper (optional)

2 tablespoons toasted sesame oil

½ cup reduced-sodium soy sauce

2 tablespoons agave nectar

¼ cup apple cider vinegar

½ cup freshly squeezed orange juice

½ teaspoon shichimi togarashi

6 bone-in, skin on chicken thighs

3 tablespoons sesame seeds

2 teaspoons cornstarch

Directions

Line a 13 by 9-inch baking pan with parchment paper. In a food processor, blend the ginger, garlic, jalapeño, sesame oil, soy sauce, agave nectar, vinegar, orange juice, and togarashi until smooth. Place the chicken in the pan, pour over the marinade, and toss to coat. Cover tightly with foil and refrigerate for at least 4 hours, but preferably over-night.

Preheat the oven to 350 degrees F.

Bake the chicken with the foil on for 30 minutes. Remove the foil and bake for another 15 to 30 minutes (depending on the size of chicken), until the skin is browned and crispy and the juices run clear when the chicken is cut with a knife. Transfer the chicken to a platter and sprinkle with the sesame seeds.

Pour the juices from the baking pan into a small saucepan. Bring to a boil. Mix the cornstarch with a little water to make a slurry and stir into the sauce. Cook for 2 minutes, until thickened. Serve with the chicken.

When you are ready to eat, let the miracle berry tablet dissolve on your tongue and then enjoy the dish.

Replacing ½ cup of sugar with 2 tablespoons of agave nectar
and the sweetness from the berry saves 66 calories per serving.

Teriyaki Chicken

MAKES 4 SERVINGS

Teriyaki sauce is loaded with sugar. In this recipe not only does removing the sugar yield a more delicious result, but the health benefits are obvious. I really love how the lemon and orange juices provide great flavors and complement the raisins perfectly.

Ingredients

4 boneless, skinless chicken breast halves

Salt and ground black pepper

½ cup reduced-sodium soy sauce

½ cup raisins

1 cup hot water

½ cup freshly squeezed orange juice

½ cup freshly squeezed lemon juice

1 teaspoon garlic powder

1 teaspoon onion powder

Canola oil spray

2 teaspoons cornstarch

Directions

Season the chicken with salt and pepper and place in a resealable plastic bag. In a blender or food processor, combine the soy sauce, raisins, water, orange juice, lemon juice, garlic powder, and onion powder. Puree until smooth. Pour into the bag over the chicken, seal the bag, and refrigerate for at least an hour, or overnight.

Preheat the oven to 350 degrees F. Cover a baking sheet with aluminum foil and spray with canola oil.

Remove the chicken from the marinade, reserving the marinade. Arrange the chicken on the baking sheet. Bake for about 30 minutes, or until cooked through and the juices run clear when the chicken is cut with a knife.

Pour the reserved marinade into a saucepan and place over medium-high heat. Bring to a boil, then turn down the heat to a simmer and cook until sauce is reduced by half. Mix the cornstarch with a little water to make a slurry and stir into the sauce. Bring back to a boil and cook until thickened. Brush onto the cooked chicken.

When you are ready to eat, let the miracle berry tablet dissolve on your tongue and then enjoy the dish.

Replacing ½ cup of sugar with the sweetness from the berry saves 96 calories per serving.

Orange Chicken

MAKES 4 SERVINGS

Sometimes you just need that satisfying crispy goodness of fried chicken. A spicy, sweet orange glaze makes this one a total winner. Here we use the lemon juice, rice vinegar, and orange juice to enhance and create a wonderful flavor while providing the sweetness for the dish.

Ingredients

1 ½ cups plus 2 tablespoons water

2 tablespoons freshly squeezed orange juice

¼ cup freshly squeezed lemon juice

⅓ cup rice vinegar

2 ½ tablespoons reduced-sodium soy sauce

1 tablespoon grated orange zest

⅓ cup honey

½ teaspoon minced fresh ginger

½ teaspoon minced garlic

2 tablespoons chopped scallion (green onion)

¼ teaspoon crushed red pepper flakes

2 boneless, skinless chicken breast halves, cut into ½-inch pieces

1 cup all-purpose flour

¼ teaspoon salt

¼ teaspoon ground black pepper

3 tablespoons olive oil

2 tablespoons cornstarch

Directions

Combine 1 ½ cups water, the orange juice, lemon juice, vinegar, and soy sauce in a saucepan over medium-high heat. Stir in the orange zest, honey ginger, garlic, scallion, and red pepper flakes. Bring to a boil. Remove from heat and cool for 10 to 15 minutes.

Place the chicken in a resealable plastic bag. When the marinade has cooled, pour 1 cup into the bag with the chicken. Reserve the remaining marinade for sauce. Seal the bag and refrigerate for at least 2 hours. (It is always a good idea to place a plastic bag with raw chicken in a rigid container, just in case of leakage. You can never be too careful when working with raw chicken!)

When you are ready to cook, mix the flour, salt, and black pepper in another resealable bag. Drain the chicken, add to the flour, seal the bag, and shake to coat.

Heat the oil in a large skillet over medium heat. Brown the chicken on both sides. Drain on a plate lined with paper towels and cover with aluminum foil to keep warm.

Wipe out the skillet and pour in the reserved marinade. Bring to a boil over medium-high heat. Mix the cornstarch and 2 tablespoons water to form a slurry. Stir into the marinade and cook until thickened. Turn down the heat to medium-low, add the chicken pieces, and simmer about 5 minutes, stirring occasionally.

When you are ready to eat, let the miracle berry tablet dissolve on your tongue and then enjoy the dish.

Replacing 1 cup of packed brown sugar with ⅓ cup of honey
and the sweetness from the berry saves 123 calories per serving.

Pork with Apples and Cider Sauce

MAKES 4 SERVINGS

Apples are already delicious, but after a miracle berry, they are spectacular. The more tart, the better. This recipe calls for Granny Smith apples, but any kind will work. Here we are using the apple cider vinegar as a replacement for any sugar we would otherwise have added.

Ingredients

3 tablespoons olive oil

2 yellow onions, sliced thin

¾ cup apple cider vinegar

¼ cup Calvados or apple brandy

1 cup skim milk

2 teaspoons cornstarch

1 tablespoon chopped fresh thyme

Salt and ground black pepper

4 boneless, center-cut pork chops, 5 ounces each

3 tablespoons all-purpose flour

3 tablespoons unsalted butter

2 tablespoons honey

3 Granny Smith apples, peeled, cored and sliced into ⅓-inch rings

1 teaspoon ground cinnamon

½ teaspoon ground nutmeg

¼ teaspoon ground cloves

Directions

In a large skillet, heat 1 tablespoon of the olive oil over medium heat. Add the onions and cook for 5 minutes, or until translucent. Remove the pan from the heat and add the apple cider and Calvados. (Stand back from the pan; alcohol can catch fire when added to a hot pan, especially if it is still over a flame.) Return the pan to the heat and cook until the liquid is syrupy. Stir in the milk, cornstarch, and thyme, and season with salt and pepper. Bring to a boil, turn down the heat to a simmer, and keep warm until ready to use.

Lay a 10-inch piece of plastic wrap on a flat work surface. Place 1 pork chop on the plastic and cover with another 10-inch piece of plastic wrap. Pound with meat mallet or heavy pan until ¼-inch thick. Repeat with remaining chops.

In a shallow baking pan, mix the flour, ½ teaspoon salt, and ¼ teaspoon black pepper. Dredge the pork in flour on both sides.

Heat the remaining 2 tablespoons oil over medium-high heat in another large skillet. When hot, carefully place 2 chops in the oil and fry until golden, about 3 minutes per side. Remove when done and add to the simmering sauce to keep warm. Repeat with the remaining chops.

In the pan in which you cooked the chops, melt the butter over medium heat. Add the honey, apples, cinnamon, nutmeg, and cloves and a pinch of salt and cook until the apples are tender, about 2 minutes per side.

Pour the warm apples over the pork chops and serve with the sauce.

When you are ready to eat, let the miracle berry tablet dissolve on your tongue and then enjoy the dish.

Replacing 1 cup of sugar with 2 tablespoons of honey
and the sweetness from the berry saves 160 calories per serving.

Pork Chops with Apricot-Chipotle Marmalade

MAKES 4 SERVINGS

I love the combination of sweet apricots and spicy chipotles in this sauce. It's also great on chicken. Since you probably won't have leftovers, make a double batch for sandwiches the next day. Chipotles pack a lot of flavor into food as well as heat, but if you can take a little more heat, definitely double the chipotles in this recipe. Our original recipe required one-third cup of sugar and here we have replaced that with the acidity in the chipotle adobo sauce.

Ingredients

Four 1-inch-thick, 6-ounce
   bone-in pork chops
Salt and ground black
   pepper
2 tablespoons olive oil
¾ cup thinly sliced shallots

1 cup dried apricots, coarsely
   chopped
1 tablespoon canned chipotle puree
   or 1 chipotle pepper in adobo
   sauce, finely chopped
2 cups low-sodium chicken broth

Directions

Preheat the oven to 350 degrees F.

Season pork chops with salt and pepper. Heat 1 tablespoon of the oil in a large ovenproof skillet over medium-high heat. When very hot, sear the pork chops for 2 to 3 minutes until golden brown, turn and sear the other side for 2 minutes until golden brown as well. Remove from the skillet and set aside on a platter.

In same skillet, heat the remaining tablespoon oil over medium heat and sauté the shallots until golden, about 2 minutes, scraping up the browned bits from the bottom of the pan. Add the apricots, chipotle puree, and broth. Bring to a boil. Turn down the heat and simmer until apricots are plumped and sauce has thickened, about 10 minutes. Add pork chops and any collected juices to the pan, cover, and bake for 15 to 20 minutes. Arrange chops on serving platter and top with the marmalade.

When you are ready to eat, let the miracle berry tablet dissolve on your tongue and then enjoy the dish.

———————

Replacing ⅓ cup of sugar with the sweetness from the berry saves 63 calories per serving.

Pork Tenderloin with Prune-Ancho Barbecue Sauce

MAKES 4 SERVINGS

Barbecue sauce with miracle berries can be a really delicious experience. In this recipe, we have a whole host of acids playing harmoniously with the ancho chiles to create a wonderfully complex and mouthwatering sauce. In this recipe, we eliminate the need for sugar by replacing it with lime juice and acidity from the tomato.

Ingredients

One 1 ½-pound pork tenderloin

Salt and ground black pepper

Olive oil

1 yellow onion, sliced

2 cloves garlic, minced

½ cup freshly squeezed orange juice

½ cup freshly squeezed lime juice

½ cup brandy

4 large dried ancho chile peppers, seeds removed

½ cup pitted prunes

1 medium tomato, quartered

½ cup low-sodium chicken broth

Directions

Preheat the oven to 375 degrees F. Line a baking sheet with aluminum foil.

Season the pork with salt and pepper. In a large skillet, heat 1 tablespoon olive oil over high heat. When the pan is very hot, sear the pork until browned on all sides. Remove from the pan and place on the baking sheet.

If pan looks dry, add another tablespoon of oil. Turn down the heat to medium, add the onion and garlic, and cook for 3 minutes, scraping up any browned bits from the bottom of the pan. Remove the pan from the heat and carefully add orange juice, lime juice and brandy. (Stand back from the pan; alcohol can catch fire when added to a hot pan, especially if it is still over a flame.) Return the pan to the heat and cook until liquid has reduced by half.

Add the anchos, prunes, tomato, and broth and bring to a boil. Turn down the heat to a simmer and cook until liquid is again reduced by half. Puree with an immersion blender in the pan or in a food processor. Strain through a fine-mesh strainer. Baste the pork with a little of the sauce. Keep the remaining sauce warm.

Insert an ovenproof digital meat thermometer into the thinnest end of the meat. Roast for 15 to 20 minutes, until internal temperature registers 135 degrees F. Remove from the oven, tent the meat with foil, and let rest for 10 minutes.

Slice the pork into ½-inch slices, and serve with the remaining sauce.

When you are ready to eat, let the miracle berry tablet dissolve on your tongue and then enjoy the dish.

———————

Replacing 1 cup of sugar with the sweetness from the berry saves 192 calories per serving.

Ribs with BBQ Sauce

MAKES 4 SERVINGS

Ribs are one of my all-time favorite foods, and spending a day smoking and grilling a rack or two produces a great product, but it's not always practical. This oven-baked recipe is something different. The resulting ribs are chewy yet tender. We have used the acidity from pineapple, tomato, and cider vinegar to remove the sugar and give this dish wonderful depth of flavor.

Ingredients

2 full slabs pork ribs, about 13 ribs per slab

1 teaspoon cayenne pepper

1 tablespoon sweet smoked paprika

1 tablespoon onion powder

1 tablespoon ground coriander

1 tablespoon ground cumin

2 tablespoons salt

1 tablespoon ground black pepper

BBQ Sauce

4 slices bacon, cut into ½-inch pieces

1 yellow onion, sliced

5 cloves garlic, sliced

1 jalapeño pepper, sliced

4 plum or Roma tomatoes, quartered

¾ cup diced fresh pineapple, in ¼-inch pieces

¼ cup apple cider vinegar

¼ cup honey

1 cup low-sodium beef broth

Directions

TO PREPARE THE RIBS: With a sharp knife, carefully remove the membrane from the bottom (nonmeaty) side of the rib racks.

Mix the cayenne, paprika, onion powder, coriander, cumin, salt, and black pepper. Reserve 2 tablespoons of the spices for the sauce. Generously spread spices over the meaty side of the slabs. Wrap the ribs tightly in plastic wrap, place in a very large, resealable plastic bag, and refrigerate. The longer the meat can sit with the rub on it, the better. Overnight is fine.

About 3 ½ hours before you want to eat, position a rack in the middle of the oven. Heat the broiler to high.

Put a broiler pan or roasting pan with a rack in the oven and carefully pour hot water into the pan, filling it ½ to 1 inch deep, so meat will not touch the water. Place the meat on the rack, meaty side down. Broil for 5 minutes with the oven door ajar; don't take your eyes off the ribs. You want the fat on the bony side to bubble and brown, but not burn. Turn over the slabs, meaty side up, turn down the oven temperature to 225 degrees F, and bake uncovered for 3 hours. Check every 30 minutes or so to add more water if the pan is dry.

TO MAKE THE SAUCE: While the ribs are baking, in a large saucepan over medium-high heat, cook the bacon until slightly browned and crisp on the edges. Add the onion, garlic, and jalapeño. Cook until the vegetables are softened, about 5 minutes. Add the tomatoes, pineapple, vinegar, honey, broth, and the reserved 2 tablespoons spices. Turn down the heat to a simmer and cook for 1 hour.

Puree until smooth with an immersion blender in the pot or in batches in a blender.

When ribs are cooked, remove from the oven and brush with the sauce. Turn the broiler back to high and broil for 2 to 5 minutes to caramelize the sauce, watching carefully so it doesn't burn. Cut the ribs into portions and serve with extra sauce.

When you are ready to eat, let the miracle berry tablet dissolve on your tongue and then enjoy the dish.

Replacing 1 cup of packed brown sugar with ¼ cup of honey
and the sweetness from the berry saves 144 calories per serving.

Asian Short Ribs

MAKES 4 SERVINGS

It's easy to see why short ribs are popping up on everyone's menus—they are fabulous, foolproof, and a real bargain. Bone-in or boneless, I love 'em every which way, especially leftovers made into a sandwich with some horseradish cream the next day!

Ingredients

1 teaspoon salt

1 tablespoon ground black pepper

1 to 2 tablespoons shichimi togarashi (Japanese spice blend; see head note, page 84)

1 to 2 tablespoons onion powder

1 to 2 tablespoons garlic powder

2 pounds boneless beef short ribs

2 tablespoons toasted sesame oil

1 yellow onion, chopped

10 cloves garlic, smashed and peeled

3 tablespoons minced fresh ginger

3 jalapeño peppers, seeded and chopped (optional)

2 carrots, peeled and sliced into ½-inch chunks

¼ cup freshly squeezed lime juice

¼ cup rice vinegar

½ cup reduced-sodium soy sauce

3 cups low-sodium beef broth

Steamed rice, for serving

Directions

In a small bowl, combine the salt, pepper, shichimi togarashi, and onion and garlic powders. Sprinkle the beef with this seasoning on all sides. In a Dutch oven, heat the sesame oil over high heat. Sear the short ribs until a brown crust forms on each side. Make sure not to crowd the pan when you are searing the meat—if the ribs touch each other, they will steam rather than sear. You may need to sear the meat in batches to get the browning needed. Remove the meat from the pan.

Add the onion, garlic, ginger, jalapeños (if using), and carrots to the hot pan. Scrap up any browned bits from the bottom the pan, and cook for 5 minutes, stirring occasionally. Add the lime juice, vinegar, soy sauce, and beef broth. Bring to a boil. Add the short ribs and any juices that may have collected. Turn down the heat to a low simmer and cook, covered, for 2 ½ hours until the beef is fork-tender. Remove the short ribs and set aside. Strain out the vegetables and discard them. Serve the ribs with just enough of the braising liquid to keep them moist, which should be approximately ¼ cup. Discard the rest. Serve ribs with steamed rice.

When you are ready to eat, let the miracle berry tablet dissolve on your tongue and then enjoy the dish.

*Replacing ½ cup of packed brown sugar
with the sweetness from the berry saves 104 calories per serving.*

Yellow Curry Beef

MAKES 4 SERVINGS

Yellow curry beef has all the qualities of a balanced dish: sweet, salt, velvety texture. Miracle berries subdue the spicy quality and but let it linger on the tongue longer. To eliminate the need for sugar, we use white wine vinegar along with acidity from the tomatoes.

Ingredients

3 pounds beef stew meat, cut into 1-inch cubes

2 teaspoons salt

6 cloves garlic, chopped

1-inch piece fresh ginger, peeled, sliced, and crushed

3 ½ tablespoons white vinegar

1 tablespoon curry powder

1 tablespoon ground black pepper

1 ½ tablespoons cayenne pepper

3 tablespoons vegetable oil

8 fresh curry leaves (these can be found at most Asian grocery stores—optional)

1 yellow onion, sliced

1 cinnamon stick

4 green cardamom pods

2 whole cloves

2 tablespoons tomato paste

1 cup low-sodium beef broth

1 cup unsweetened coconut milk

Directions

Rinse the beef and pat dry with paper towel.

On a cutting board, sprinkle the salt over the garlic and using the side of your knife, mash the salt into the garlic, creating a paste. Add the ginger and incorporate into the mix with your knife. Transfer the paste to a large bowl. Stir in the vinegar, curry powder, black pepper, and cayenne. Add the beef cubes and toss to coat. Marinate for 30 minutes.

Heat the oil in a Dutch oven over medium heat. Stir in the curry leaves, if using, then the onion. Cook for 5 minutes, stirring frequently, until the onion has softened and is translucent. Add the beef and brown on all sides, about 10 minutes. Stir in the cinnamon stick, cardamom pods, cloves, tomato paste, and broth. Turn down the heat to low and cook, covered, for 1 ½ hours or until the meat is tender. Check the curry after 30 minutes to make sure there is enough liquid to braise the beef. If it looks like it might stick to the pan, add up to 1 cup of water.

Stir in the coconut milk and heat through. Remove the cinnamon stick, taste, and adjust the salt and pepper before serving.

When you are ready to eat, let the miracle berry tablet dissolve on your tongue and then enjoy the dish.

Replacing ½ cup of sugar with the sweetness from the berry saves 96 calories per serving.

Korean Beef with Quick Kim Chi and Spicy Sambal

MAKES 4 SERVINGS

Just for fun, try some sambal by itself after eating a miracle berry. You'll still taste the heat, but you'll also taste the peppers themselves, which doesn't often happen with spicy foods. It's a great balance to the sweet beef and tangy kim chi.

Korean Beef

4 scallions (green onions), coarsely chopped

6 cloves garlic, peeled

1-inch piece fresh ginger, peeled and chopped

1 cup reduced-sodium soy sauce

1 tablespoon honey

¼ cup freshly squeezed lemon juice

½ cup toasted sesame oil

2 pounds boneless beef short ribs, sliced thinly against the grain

Kim Chi

1 tablespoon vegetable or peanut oil

1 tablespoon toasted sesame oil

1 head napa cabbage, thinly sliced

1 clove garlic, minced

¼ cup apple cider vinegar

½ cup reduced-sodium soy sauce

1 tablespoon crushed red pepper flakes

3 scallions (green onions), sliced thinly

¾ cup toasted sesame seeds

Spicy Sambal

2 stalks lemongrass

1 tomato, chopped

1 cup chopped jalapeños, with seeds

½ yellow onion, chopped

10 cloves garlic, peeled and
    crushed

1 tablespoon XO shrimp paste

(this can be found at most
    Asian grocery stores)

2 tablespoons honey

2 tablespoons freshly squeezed lime
    juice

2 tablespoons salt

2 tablespoons vegetable oil

Directions

TO MARINATE THE BEEF: In a food processor, mix the scallions, garlic, ginger, soy sauce, honey, lemon juice, and sesame oil. Blend until smooth. Pour over the beef in a large bowl, turn the meat to coat, cover, and refrigerate for 2 to 24 hours.

TO MAKE THE KIM CHI: Heat the vegetable and sesame oils in a large saucepan over medium heat. Add the cabbage and cook until softened, about 5 minutes. Stir in the garlic and vinegar and turn down the heat to low. Cover and cook for 20 minutes. Remove from the heat and stir in the soy sauce, red pepper flakes, scallions, and sesame seeds. Store in covered pot until the rest of the dish is ready to serve.

TO MAKE THE SAMBAL: Remove the tough outer leaves from the lemongrass stalks. Cut the main yellow stem into 2- to 3-inch lengths and bruise with the back of a knife or bend them several times. In a blender or food processor, combine the lemongrass, tomato, jalapeños, onion, garlic, shrimp paste, honey, lime juice, salt, and oil. Transfer to a large saucepan and cook until fragrant. Strain through a fine mesh strainer to remove all pulp and refrigerate until serving. Strained sauce should have a smooth consistency. If not, then restrain.

When ready to cook, heat a grill to high. Let the meat come to room temperature. Remove the meat from the marinade and dry with paper towels. Grill for 1 to 2 minutes per side, allowing some black charring on the edges of the meat before turning. Serve with kim chi and sambal on the side.

When you are ready to eat, let the miracle berry tablet dissolve on your tongue and then enjoy the dish.

———————

Replacing ½ cup of sugar from the beef, kim chi, and sambal with 3 tablespoons of honey and the sweetness from the berry saves 48 calories per serving.

Collard Greens with Ham Hocks

MAKES 4 SERVINGS

I learned how to make collard greens from my friend Reggie. They were delicious, but loaded with butter and sugar, which kind of defeats the purpose of a vegetable. You won't miss the sugar and butter in this recipe—it's better than the original.

Ingredients

1 bunch collard greens, heavy stems removed, leaves trimmed and chopped

2 smoked ham hocks

2 ½ cups low-sodium chicken broth

2 ½ cups water

1 tablespoon balsamic vinegar

Salt and ground black pepper

Directions

Place the collard greens and ham hocks in a large pot. Cover with the broth, water, and vinegar. Season with salt and pepper. Bring to a boil, turn down the heat to low, cover, and simmer 1 to 1 ½ hours. Remove from pot and serve.

When you are ready to eat, let the miracle berry tablet dissolve on your tongue and then enjoy the dish.

Replacing ⅓ cup of packed brown sugar with the sweetness from the berry saves 70 calories per serving.

Candied Jalapeños

If you have never enjoyed this Southern classic, you must. They are really tasty and a great accompaniment to any of the barbecued dishes in this book.

Ingredients

1 ½ cups apple cider vinegar

¼ cup honey

20 raw jalapeño peppers, thinly sliced

Directions

Bring the vinegar and honey to a boil in a large saucepan over high heat. Cook and stir until the honey has dissolved. Add the jalapeños and remove from the heat. Let stand for 1 hour. Cool to room temperature before serving or store in the refrigerator in an airtight container.

When you are ready to eat, let the miracle berry tablet dissolve on your tongue and then enjoy the dish.

Replacing 1 cup of sugar with ¼ cup of honey and the sweetness from the berry saves 64 to 86 calories per serving.

Southwestern Coleslaw

MAKES 8 SERVINGS

Classic coleslaw has a slightly sweet flavor and crunchy texture with a little richness from the mayonnaise. With miracle berries, we use vinegar for sweetness and are able to cut the sugar altogether. Bacon is an optional ingredient in this recipe. If possible, try to find bacon made without sugar, or substitute rendered pancetta or peppered pork belly.

Ingredients

2 ears fresh corn, shucked, silk removed

½ teaspoon vegetable oil

1 ½ cups mayonnaise

¼ cup apple cider vinegar

2 tablespoons ground cumin

1 tablespoon salt

½ teaspoon ground black pepper

1 medium-size head cabbage, cut into ⅛-inch ribbons

1 carrot, grated

1 can black beans, rinsed and drained

5 slices bacon, diced and cooked until browned and crispy

Directions

Heat a grill pan over high heat. Brush corn with the oil and grill for 5 minutes on each side, until corn is slightly blackened and caramelized. Set aside. When cool enough to handle, slice the kernels off cobs. (My wife, Katie, uses a Bundt pan to hold the ears of corn as she cuts off the kernels—it catches all of the corn without making a mess. Pretty smart!) Hold at room temperature until serving.

In a blender or food processor, combine the mayonnaise, vinegar, cumin, salt, and pepper. Toss with the cabbage and carrot in a large bowl and refrigerate for several hours or overnight.

When ready to serve, stir in the beans, bacon, and corn kernels. Check for seasoning, adding more salt and/or pepper if necessary.

When you are ready to eat, let the miracle berry tablet dissolve on your tongue and then enjoy the dish.

———————————

Replacing ½ cup sugar with the sweetness from the berry saves 48 calories per serving.

DESSERTS

Lemon Poppy Seed Cake with Goat Cheese Frosting

This is an unexpected pairing in a dessert—lemon and goat cheese . . . but with a miracle berry, absolutely amazing. For this cake, we have used the natural acidity from the lemon to add sweetness, and we eliminated the sugar.

Ingredients

Canola oil spray

3 ¾ cups cake flour (see note)

3 tablespoons baking powder

1 tablespoon salt

6 large eggs

1 cup whole milk

½ cup freshly squeezed lemon juice

2 tablespoons grated lemon zest

¼ cup honey

¼ cup poppy seeds

1 recipe Goat Cheese Frosting
  (page 269)

Directions

Preheat the oven to 350 degrees F. Spray a 10-inch Bundt pan with canola oil.

Sift the flour and baking powder into a large bowl. In another bowl, whip the eggs until bubbly. Add the milk, lemon juice, lemon zest, honey and poppy seeds, whipping for another 3 minutes until light and fluffy. Carefully fold the wet ingredients into the flour until incorporated.

Pour the batter into the Bundt pan and bake for 25 minutes or until a toothpick inserted into the middle comes out clean.

Cool for 30 minutes in the pan on a wire rack. Invert the cake onto a wire rack to cool completely. Drizzle with Goat Cheese Frosting and serve.

NOTE: If you don't have cake flour, you can make your own. For every cup of cake flour needed, place 2 tablespoons of cornstarch in a 1-cup measure, then fill the rest of the cup with all-purpose flour. Sift the ingredients a few times to aerate the mixture.

When you are ready to eat, let the miracle berry tablet dissolve on your tongue and then enjoy the dish.

Replacing 2 cups of sugar with ¼ cup of honey and the sweetness from the berry saves 160 calories per serving.
The Goat Cheese Frosting saves an additional 51 calories per serving, for a total of 179 calories per serving.

Over-the-Top Lemon Layer Cake

MAKES ONE 9-INCH LAYER CAKE (10 SERVINGS)

The name says it all. A moist light cake that's filled with homemade lemon curd is over the top.

Ingredients

Canola oil spray

2 ½ cups whole-wheat flour

½ teaspoon salt

1 tablespoon baking powder

1 cup skim milk

1 cup vegetable oil

1 teaspoon pure vanilla extract

1 tablespoon grated lemon zest

4 large eggs

½ cup agave nectar

1 recipe Lemon Curd (page 252)

1 recipe Lemon Buttercream Frosting
    (page 266)

Directions

Position a rack in the middle of the oven and preheat the oven to 350 degrees F. Spray two 9-inch cake pans with canola oil. Line the bottom of each pan with a round of parchment or wax paper and spray the paper.

Whisk together the flour, salt, and baking powder. In a separate bowl, combine the milk, vegetable oil, vanilla, and lemon zest.

With an electric mixer, beat together the eggs and agave nectar until combined, about 1 minute. Turn down the mixer speed to low and add the flour and milk mixtures alternately, beginning and ending with flour. Mix until just combined.

Divide the batter evenly between the pans, and smooth the tops. Bake for 35 to 40 minutes, until a toothpick inserted in center of each cake layer comes out clean.

Cool the cake layers in the pans on wire racks for 10 minutes. Run a thin knife around edge of each cake pan and invert cakes onto the racks to cool completely.

To assemble the cake, slice each cake layer in half horizontally using a long serrated knife. Spread the bottom half of each layer with half of the lemon curd, then top with remaining cake layers to form two sandwiched cakes. Place one sandwiched cake on a cake stand or platter and spread with ½ cup of the frosting. Top with the other sandwiched cake. Frost the top and sides of cake with the remaining frosting.

NOTE: Cake layers can be made a day ahead and cooled completely, then wrapped tightly in plastic wrap and kept at room temperature. The lemon curd can be stored for up to 3 days in the refrigerator. The frosted cake can be covered loosely with plastic wrap and refrigerated for up to 1 day. Bring to room temperature before serving.

When you are ready to eat, let the miracle berry tablet dissolve on your tongue and then enjoy the dish.

Replacing 2 cups of sugar from the cake, with ½ cup of agave nectar
and the sweetness from the berry saves 106 calories per serving.
The Buttercream Frosting saves an additional 62 calories per serving,
and the Lemon Curd saves an additional 34 calories per serving,
for a total of 202 calories saved per serving.

Tres Leches Cake

MAKES ONE 13 BY 9-INCH CAKE (12 SERVINGS)

This cake is pure heaven. I love how the grapefruit, lemon, and lime juice works perfectly with the mascarpone to create a wonderfully sweetened and moist cake.

Ingredients

Canola oil spray

1 cup unbleached all-purpose flour

1 ½ teaspoons baking powder

¼ teaspoon salt

4 large eggs, separated

¼ cup agave nectar

1 teaspoon pure vanilla extract

⅔ cup freshly squeezed grapefruit juice

⅓ cup freshly squeezed lime juice

⅓ cup grated lemon zest

1 recipe Mascarpone Frosting (page 268)

Directions

Preheat the oven to 350 degrees F. Spray a 13 by 9-inch baking pan with canola oil.

Combine the flour, baking powder, and salt in a large bowl. In a separate bowl, beat the egg yolks with 2 tablespoons of the agave nectar on high speed until pale yellow. Stir in the vanilla, ⅓ cup of the grapefruit juice and the lime juice. Add to the flour and gently combine.

With an electric mixer, beat the egg whites on high speed until soft peaks form. With the mixer running, add the remaining 2 tablespoons agave nectar and beat until egg whites are stiff but not dry. Fold in the lemon zest. Gently fold egg whites into the rest of the batter, being careful not to deflate the egg whites. Pour into the pan and smooth the top.

Bake for 35 to 45 minutes or until a toothpick comes out clean. Invert the cake onto a rimmed platter and allow to cool.

When cake is cool, pierce the surface with a fork several times. Slowly drizzle the remaining ⅓ cup grapefruit juice onto the top and down the sides of the cake. Let the cake absorb the juice for 30 minutes.

Frost the cake with Mascarpone Frosting.

When you are ready to eat, let the miracle berry tablet dissolve on your tongue and then enjoy the dish.

Replacing 2 cups of sugar from the cake and frosting with 7 tablespoons of agave nectar and the sweetness from the berry saves 93 calories per serving.

Pineapple Zucchini Cake

MAKES ONE 13 BY 9-INCH CAKE (12 SERVINGS)

Pineapples are naturally sweet. With miracle berries they are slightly sweeter, which enables this cake to lose some sugar from the original recipe—and with the grapefruit juice, the cake balances out nicely.

Ingredients

Canola oil spray

1 cup unbleached all-purpose flour

½ cup whole-wheat flour

½ cup unsweetened flaked coconut

2 teaspoons baking soda

1 teaspoon salt

2 teaspoons ground cinnamon

¼ teaspoon ground nutmeg

¼ teaspoon ground ginger

3 tablespoons vegetable oil

1 large egg

1 ¼ cups agave nectar

1 teaspoon pure vanilla extract

½ cup freshly squeezed grapefruit juice

2 cups grated zucchini (see note)

3 cups chopped fresh pineapple (reserve any pineapple juice)

1 recipe Vanilla Frosting (page 265)

Directions

Preheat the oven to 350 degrees F. Spray a 13 by 9-inch baking pan with canola oil.

In a large bowl, whisk together the all-purpose and whole-wheat flours, coconut, baking soda, salt, cinnamon, nutmeg, and ginger. In a separate bowl, combine the vegetable oil, egg, agave nectar, vanilla, and grapefruit juice. Stir in the zucchini and pineapple and fold into the flour. The batter may be stiff, but keep folding until it comes together. If it is too dry, add a few drops of the reserved pineapple juice to moisten it slightly.

Spoon batter into the pan. Bake for 33 to 35 minutes, until a toothpick inserted in the center comes out clean. Cool completely in the pan on a wire rack.

Frost with Vanilla Frosting.

NOTE: If your zucchini are particularly large, scoop out the seeds before grating, and spread on a layer of paper towels to drain any excess water before adding to the batter.

When you are ready to eat, let the miracle berry tablet dissolve on your tongue and then enjoy the dish.

Replacing 1 ½ cups of sugar from the Vanilla Frosting with ¼ cup of agave nectar and the sweetness from the berry, plus replacing 3 ¼ cups of sugar from the cake with 1 ¼ cups of agave nectar and the sweetness from the berry saves 168 calories per serving.

Crunchy Polenta Cake with Strawberries

While this may seem like a pretty upscale dessert, the flavors are comforting and familiar. The balsamic vinegar and strawberries marry perfectly with the polenta and lime. The perfect Italian dessert, it's certain to become a family favorite.

Strawberries

1 cup balsamic vinegar

1 pint strawberries, stemmed and quartered

2 tablespoons agave nectar

2 sprigs rosemary

¼ cup shredded fresh mint leaves

Cake

Canola oil spray

3 ½ cups unbleached all-purpose flour, plus more for the pan

1 cup polenta (coarse yellow cornmeal)

1 tablespoon baking powder

¼ teaspoon salt

¾ pound (3 sticks) unsalted butter, melted

⅓ cups agave nectar

4 large eggs, beaten

1 cup freshly squeezed grapefruit juice

Grated zest of 6 limes

Fresh mint sprigs, for garnish

Directions

FOR THE STRAWBERRIES: Slowly heat the vinegar to a simmer. Transfer to a bowl and stir in the strawberries, agave nectar, rosemary, and mint. Cover with plastic wrap and let sit at room temperature for a few hours. (Heating the vinegar will help release the essential oils from the rosemary and mint.)

TO MAKE THE CAKE: Preheat the oven to 325 degrees F. Spray a 9-inch square baking pan with canola oil and sprinkle with flour, tapping out the excess.

In a large bowl, combine the flour, polenta, baking powder, and salt. Make a well in the center. In a separate bowl, combine butter and agave nectar. Stir in the eggs, grapefruit juice, and lime zest. Pour into the well in the flour and mix until combined. Transfer the batter to the pan and smooth the top.

Bake for 25 minutes or until toothpick inserted in the center of the cake comes out clean. Cool on a wire rack. Turn up the oven temperature to 350 degrees F.

When the cake is completely cool, cut into 1-inch cubes and spread on a baking sheet. Bake for 5 minutes.

Drain the strawberries, discarding the rosemary and all but ¼ cup of the liquid. Serve the cake cubes with the berries and garnish with mint sprigs or store refrigerated, covered in plastic.

When you are ready to eat, let the miracle berry tablet dissolve on your tongue and then enjoy the dish.

Replacing 1 ⅛ cups of sugar with about 7 tablespoons of agave nectar
and the sweetness from the berry saves 53 calories per serving.

Chocolate Guinness Cake

MAKES 12 SERVINGS

I adapted this cake from one we serve at the restaurant. You must try the Guinness stout with the miracle berry alone. Most people describe it as the best chocolate milk they've ever tasted, so it seemed like the perfect match. The beer actually provides the sweetness, along with the sour cream. A very delicious and unique experience.

Ingredients

½ pound (2 sticks) unsalted butter, plus 1 tablespoon for the pan

1 tablespoon unsweetened Dutch-process cocoa powder

2 ½ cups unbleached all-purpose flour

¾ teaspoon baking soda

½ teaspoon kosher salt

¾ cup stout (such as Guinness)

½ cup freshly squeezed lime juice

2 cups chopped unsweetened chocolate

2 large eggs

½ cup agave nectar

½ cup low-fat sour cream

½ cup heavy cream

Directions

Preheat the oven to 350 degrees F. Grease a 12-cup Bundt pan with 1 tablespoon of the butter and dust with the cocoa powder, tapping out the excess.

In a medium bowl, whisk together the flour, baking soda, and salt. In a small saucepan, heat the remaining ½ pound of butter, the stout, and lime juice over medium heat until butter is melted. Remove from heat, add half of the chocolate, and whisk until smooth.

With an electric mixer, beat the eggs and agave nectar on medium-high speed until combined. Beat in the chocolate mixture and the sour cream. Turn down the mixer speed to low and gradually mix in the flour until just combined; do not overmix.

Pour the batter into the pan and bake for 45 to 55 minutes, until a toothpick inserted in the center comes out with a few moist crumbs attached. Let cool 30 minutes in the pan, then invert onto a wire rack to cool completely.

In a small saucepan, bring the heavy cream to just below boiling, about 180 degrees F. Remove from heat, add the remaining chocolate, and let sit 5 minutes. Whisk until smooth. Set the wire rack with the cake over a baking sheet. Drizzle the cake with the glaze. Allow the glaze to harden slightly before serving or keep covered in plastic in the refrigerator.

When you are ready to eat, let the miracle berry tablet dissolve on your tongue and then enjoy the dish.

*Replacing 2 cups of sugar with ½ cup of agave nectar
and the sweetness of the berry saves 88 calories per serving.*

Red Velvet Sheet Cake

MAKES ONE 18 BY 12-INCH CAKE (12 SERVINGS)

I am opposed to using red food coloring, so in this recipe I use pure pomegranate juice. With its tart profile, it adds a little sweetening along with the lemon juice to create the red velvet cake flavor we all know and love.

Ingredients

Canola oil spray

2 ½ cups cake flour (see note)

1 ¼ teaspoon salt

1 cup low-fat buttermilk

1 large egg

1 teaspoon pure vanilla extract

1 teaspoon baking soda

1 ½ teaspoons white vinegar

¾ cup freshly squeezed lime juice

1 ½ teaspoons unsweetened Dutch-process cocoa powder

⅓ cup freshly squeezed lemon juice

3 tablespoons unsweetened pomegranate juice

1 cup vegetable shortening

½ cup agave nectar

1 recipe Cream Cheese Frosting (page 267)

Directions

Preheat the oven to 350 degrees F. Spray an 18 by 12-inch jelly-roll pan with canola oil.

Sift together the flour and salt. In a separate bowl, combine the buttermilk, egg, vanilla, and baking soda. Stir in the vinegar and lime juice. In another bowl, combine the cocoa, lemon juice, and pomegranate juice. With an electric mixer, beat shortening and agave nectar until fluffy. Alternate stirring in the flour and the buttermilk-egg mixture. Add the cocoa mixture and beat until combined.

Pour the batter into the pan and smooth the surface. Bake for 20 minutes.

Let the cake cool in the pan for 20 minutes. Invert the cake onto a cutting board. Frost with Cream Cheese Frosting.

NOTE: If you don't have cake flour, you can make your own. For every cup of cake flour needed, place 2 tablespoons of cornstarch in a 1-cup measure, then fill the rest of the cup with all-purpose flour. Sift the ingredients a few times to aerate the mixture.

When you are ready to eat, let the miracle berry tablet dissolve on your tongue and then enjoy the dish.

Replacing ½ cup sugar with ½ cup of agave nectar
and the sweetness from the berry saves 56 calories per serving.
The Cream Cheese Frosting replaces 2 ¾ cups of sugar with 2 tablespoons of agave nectar
and the sweetness from the berry saving 167 calories per serving,
for a total of 223 calories saved per serving.

Molten Chocolate Cakes

MAKES 4 INDIVIDUAL CAKES (4 SERVINGS)

If chocolate and raspberries are the perfect marriage, then chocolate, raspberries, and miracle berries are the perfect threesome. This recipe is arguably one of the very best liquid-center chocolate cakes I've ever had. Total. Crowd. Pleaser.

Ingredients

- 8 tablespoons (1 stick) unsalted butter, plus more for the ramekins
- 2 teaspoons unbleached all-purpose flour, plus more for the ramekins
- 2 ounces unsweetened chocolate, chopped
- ¼ cup Raspberry Jam (page 256)
- 2 large eggs
- 2 large egg yolks
- ¼ cup agave nectar
- Whipped Cream (page 250), optional
- Fresh raspberries (optional)

Directions

Preheat the oven to 450 degrees F. Butter and flour four 4-ounce ramekins.

In the top of a double boiler set over simmering water, heat the butter, chocolate, and jam until chocolate is almost completely melted.

In a bowl, beat the eggs, egg yolks, and agave nectar until light colored and thick. Stir the chocolate and slowly pour into the egg mixture. Add the flour and mix until just combined.

Pour the batter into the ramekins and bake for 8 to 9 minutes. The centers of the cakes will still be quite soft. Invert the cakes on serving plates and let sit for about 15 seconds, then unmold. Serve immediately with whipped cream and fresh raspberries, if desired.

When you are ready to eat, let the miracle berry tablet dissolve on your tongue and then enjoy the dish.

Replacing 1 ½ cups of sugar with ¼ cup of agave nectar and the sweetness from the berry saves 223 calories with the whipped cream, 228 without, per serving.

Chocolate Walnut Torte with Coconut Crust

Dessert is all about texture, in my opinion. This one combines the velvety texture you love about cheesecake with the crunch of walnuts swirled through it, plus a crunchy coconut crust. Way better than traditional cheesecake.

Crust

1 cup unsweetened shredded coconut

1 cup walnuts

2 tablespoons unsalted butter, softened

Chocolate Filling

⅓ cup unsweetened Dutch-process cocoa powder

¼ cup freshly squeezed lemon juice

16 ounces reduced-fat cream cheese

2 cups cold heavy cream

Walnut Filling

1 cup walnuts

⅓ cup honey

2 tablespoons canola oil

1 teaspoon salt

Garnish

2 tablespoons toasted unsweetened coconut

1 tablespoon unsweetened Dutch-process cocoa powder

Directions

TO MAKE THE CRUST: In a food processor, combine the coconut, walnuts, and butter. Pulse until the mixture resembles fine crumbs. Line the bottom of a 9-inch springform pan with parchment paper. Pour the crust into the bottom of the pan and press down with the bottom of a glass until well compressed.

TO MAKE THE CHOCOLATE FILLING: In the bowl of an electric stand mixer fitted with a whip, beat the cocoa, lemon juice, cream cheese, and cream until stiff peaks form.

TO MAKE THE WALNUT FILLING: In a food processor, combine the walnuts, honey, canola oil, and salt. Pulse until coarsely chopped, but still chunky.

Spoon half of the chocolate filling into the crust. Gently spread the walnut filling on top. Cover with the remaining chocolate filling. Refrigerate for at least 1 hour.

When ready to serve, release the sides of pan and remove. Garnish by carefully pressing the toasted coconut into the sides and sifting cocoa on top of the torte.

When you are ready to eat, let the miracle berry tablet dissolve on your tongue and then enjoy the dish.

———————

Replacing 3 cups of sugar with ⅓ cup of honey and the sweetness from the berry saves 246 calories per serving.

Tropical Fruit Skewers with Sweet Yogurt Dipping Sauce

MAKES 4 SKEWERS

This is an übersimple way to make an average fruit dessert exciting. This really takes advantage of the effect of the miracle berry on nonfat yogurt and lemon juice. The combination with the berry provides an almost sweet creamy profile that makes the fruit sing. This dish also does well as a side dish to some of the cocktails in this book.

Ingredients

1 pineapple, peeled, cored, and cut into 1-inch cubes

1 papaya, peeled, seeded, and cut into 1-inch cubes

2 bananas, peeled and cut into 1-inch pieces

2 mangos, peeled, pitted, and cut into 1-inch cubes

1 cup plain nonfat yogurt

Grated zest and juice of 1 lemon

Directions

Place fruit pieces onto wooden skewers, alternating fruit with each piece. Combine the yogurt, lemon zest, and lemon juice. Serve alongside the skewers.

When you are ready to eat, let the miracle berry tablet dissolve on your tongue and then enjoy the dish.

———————————

*Replacing ⅓ cup of sugar from the yogurt sauce
with the sweetness from the berry saves 64 calories per serving.*

Apple Crisp

Every fall, I take my family to Michigan and we pick the most wonderful apples. We are very fortunate to be so close to this amazing product when it's in season. Even if you don't have access to the freshest local apples, the miracle berry will make any apple taste better. For baking, I prefer Granny Smith, Jonagold, or Honeycrisp apples.

Ingredients

6 tart apples (such as Granny Smith, Jonagold, or Honeycrisp)

3 tablespoons honey

¼ teaspoon ground cinnamon

¼ teaspoon ground nutmeg

⅛ teaspoon ground cloves

¼ cup rice flour

⅛ teaspoon salt

3 tablespoons almond meal (finely ground blanched almonds)

2 tablespoons unsweetened shredded coconut

1 ½ tablespoons unsalted butter or margarine, softened

Directions

Preheat the oven to 375 degrees F.

Peel, core, and slice the apples. Toss the apples with the honey, cinnamon, nutmeg, and cloves. Pour into 13 × 9-inch baking pan.

Combine the rice flour, salt, almond meal, and coconut. Cut in butter until the mixture is fine and crumbly. Sprinkle over the apples.

Cover with aluminum foil and bake for 1 hour. Remove the foil and continue to bake until crumble is crisp and golden in color, about 10 minutes. Store in refrigerator covered in plastic.

When you are ready to eat, let the miracle berry tablet dissolve on your tongue and then enjoy the dish.

———————————

Replacing 1 cup of packed brown sugar with 3 tablespoons of honey and the sweetness from the berry saves 107 calories per serving.

Strawberry Shortcake

This is a classic for a reason. Very easy to make, and the lemon juice provides this recipe with more than enough sweetness.

Strawberry Topping

1 ½ cups sliced fresh strawberries

1 tablespoon freshly squeezed lemon juice

Shortcakes

1 cup unbleached all-purpose flour, plus more for rolling the dough

¾ teaspoon baking powder

⅛ teaspoon salt

2 tablespoons unsalted butter, frozen

3 tablespoons skim milk

1 large egg yolk, beaten

¾ teaspoon grated lemon zest

2 tablespoons agave nectar

Lemon Butter

1 tablespoon unsalted butter, softened   ¼ teaspoon grated lemon zest

Whipped Cream (see page 250)

Directions

Preheat the oven to 400 degrees F.

TO MAKE THE TOPPING: Combine the strawberries and lemon juice. Cover and refrigerate until serving.

TO MAKE THE SHORTCAKES: Combine the flour, baking powder, and salt. Cut in butter with fork or pastry blender until the mixture resembles coarse crumbs. Combine the milk, egg yolk, lemon zest, and agave nectar. Stir into the crumb mixture until a soft, sticky dough forms. Turn out onto a lightly floured surface; knead 10 times. Divide the dough into quarters. Gently pat or roll each piece into a ¾-inch-thick circle. Place 2 inches apart on an ungreased baking sheet. Bake for 8 to 10 minutes, until golden brown.

Transfer to a wire rack; cool for 15 minutes.

TO MAKE THE LEMON BUTTER: In a small bowl, combine the butter and lemon zest.

TO ASSEMBLE THE SHORTCAKES: Split the shortcakes horizontally in half and spread with lemon butter. Top with strawberries, the shortcake top, and a dollop of whipped cream.

When you are ready to eat, let the miracle berry tablet dissolve on your tongue and then enjoy the dish.

Replacing ½ cup of sugar in the whipped cream, ¼ cup of sugar in the strawberry topping,
and ¼ cup of sugar from the shortcakes with the sweetness from the berry
saves 147 calories per serving.
Replacing ½ cup of sugar with 2 tablespoons of agave nectar
and the sweetness from the berry saves 66 calories per serving.
Using our Whipped Cream instead of conventional whipped cream
saves an additional 20 calories per serving, for a total of 86 calories saved per serving.

Sweet Pie Crust

Ingredients

8 tablespoons (1 stick) unsalted butter, frozen and diced

3 tablespoons vegetable shortening, frozen and grated

2 ½ cups unbleached all-purpose flour

2 tablespoons agave nectar

½ cup freshly squeezed lemon juice, cold

Directions

Cut shortening and butter into the flour with a fork or pastry blender. Stir in the agave nectar and lemon juice just until dough forms. Divide the dough into two equal parts. Transfer each to a large sheet of plastic wrap. Pulling up the sides, flatten the dough into a disk. Refrigerate for at least 30 minutes before rolling.

When you are ready to eat, let the miracle berry tablet dissolve on your tongue and then enjoy the dish.

---

*Replacing ¼ cup of sugar with 2 tablespoons of agave nectar
and the sweetness from the berry saves 72 calories.*

Peach Hand Pies

These simple pies pair two classic friends: peaches and Scotch whiskey. The sweetness from the malt vinegar lends that extra layer of flavor, while complementing the peaches. If you can't find ripe peaches, don't worry—the miracle berry will make even unripe ones taste amazing in this recipe.

Ingredients

2 pounds ripe peaches

2 tablespoons agave nectar

Pinch of salt

¼ cup malt vinegar

2 tablespoons Scotch whiskey

1 large egg

1 tablespoon water

Flour, for rolling the pastry

1 recipe Sweet Pie Crust (page 132)

Directions

Bring a large pot of water to a boil. Fill a large bowl with ice and water.

Cut a small X in the bottom of each peach and place in the boiling water for 2 minutes. Remove the peaches with a slotted spoon and submerge in the ice water. When cool, slip the skins off peaches. Cut the peaches in half, remove the pits, and cut the peaches into ½-inch pieces.

Combine the peaches in a saucepan with the agave nectar, salt, vinegar, and Scotch. Cook over medium heat for 20 minutes, stirring occasionally to prevent sticking. Remove from the heat and let cool.

Preheat the oven to 350 degrees F. Line a baking sheet with parchment paper.

Beat the egg and water to make egg wash. On a lightly floured work surface, roll out the pie crust to about ⅛ of an inch thick. Cut eight 5-inch circles. Place 3 tablespoons of filling in the center of each dough circle. Brush the edges of the dough with egg wash, fold the dough over, and seal with a fork, crimping the edges. Brush the tops with egg wash and place on the baking sheet. Bake for 15 minutes, or until golden. Store in refrigerator covered in plastic.

When you are ready to eat, let the miracle berry tablet dissolve on your tongue and then enjoy the dish.

———————

Replacing ¼ cup of sugar and ¾ cup of packed brown sugar with 2 tablespoons of agave nectar and the sweetness from the berry saves 87 calories per serving.

Cardamom Apple Pie

MAKES ONE 9-INCH PIE (8 SERVINGS)

Apples and cardamom are good friends—tart and spicy. Miracle berries are perfect with the tartness of the apples, eliminating the need for sugar.

Ingredients

2 tablespoons all-purpose flour, plus more for rolling the dough

1 recipe Sweet Pie Crust (page 132)

6 tart apples (such as Granny Smith, Jonathan, Jonagold, or McIntosh)

2 teaspoons ground cinnamon

1 tablespoon ground cardamom

1 teaspoon ground nutmeg

3 tablespoons unsalted butter, cut into ¼-inch cubes

Directions

Preheat the oven to 350 degrees F.

On a lightly floured surface, roll out one dough to a circle of 12 inches in diameter. Roll the other disk slightly larger. Place the smaller circle in a 9-inch pie plate and gently tamp it down. Prick with a fork, 2 inches apart.

Peel, core and slice the apples into a large bowl. Add the cinnamon, cardamom, nutmeg, 2 tablespoons flour, and half of butter pieces. Stir to evenly coat the apples with the spices. Pour into the crust. Scatter with the rest of the butter pieces. Cover with top crust. Seal and crimp edges with a fork or your fingers. Cut steam vents in the top crust.

Bake for 45 to 55 minutes, until crust is golden brown. After 30 minutes, if edges of the crust are starting to brown, cover the edges with foil for the remainder of baking.

Allow pie to cool before cutting. Store in refrigerator covered in plastic.

When you are ready to eat, let the miracle berry tablet dissolve on your tongue and then enjoy the dish.

Replacing 2 ⅛ cups of sugar in the filling with the sweetness from the berry, plus ¼ cup of sugar from the Sweet Pie Crust with 2 tablespoons of agave nectar and the sweetness from the berry saves 213 calories per serving.

Shortbread-Topped Strawberry Pie

MAKES ONE 9-INCH PIE (8 SERVINGS)

With miracle berries, strawberries alone are intensely sweet. Here, we add the light acidity of grapefruit juice to allow the flavor of the strawberries come through, while not overpowering them with too much acidic sweetness.

Ingredients

- 3 ¾ cups unbleached all-purpose flour, plus more for rolling the dough
- ½ recipe Sweet Pie Crust (page 132)
- ¼ cup plus 2 tablespoons agave nectar
- 6 tablespoons (¾ stick) unsalted butter, softened
- 2 extra-large eggs, at room temperature
- 1 teaspoon pure vanilla extract
- 1 tablespoon grated lemon zest
- ⅓ cup freshly squeezed grapefruit juice
- 1 teaspoon baking powder
- ¼ teaspoon baking soda
- ½ teaspoon kosher salt
- 1 cup fresh strawberries
- 10 tablespoons plus 2 teaspoons (1 ⅓ sticks) unsalted butter, diced
- 1 teaspoon ground cinnamon

Directions

On a lightly floured surface, roll out the dough to a circle of 12 inches in diameter. Place the circle in a 9-inch pie plate and gently tamp it down. Crimp the edge with your fingers or a fork.

In a large bowl, mix ¼ cup of the agave nectar and the softened butter until combined. Add the eggs one at a time, stirring after each egg until combined. Stir in the vanilla, lemon zest, and grapefruit juice.

In a separate bowl, mix 1 ¼ cups of the flour, the baking powder, baking soda, and salt. Fold into the egg mixture. Cut the strawberries into quarters and stir into the filling. Pour into the pie crust.

In a food processor, combine the remaining 2 ½ cups flour and the cinnamon. Add the remaining 2 tablespoons agave nectar and the diced butter. Pulse until butter is the size of peas and the mixture is crumbly. Sprinkle over the top of the pie. Freeze the pie for 1 hour.

Preheat the oven to 350 degrees F.

Bake the pie for 30 minutes or until the edges are golden brown.

When you are ready to eat, let the miracle berry tablet dissolve on your tongue and then enjoy the dish.

---

*Replacing 1 cup of sugar from the filling and crumble
with 6 tablespoons of agave nectar and the sweetness from the berry,
plus replacing the 2 tablespoons of sugar from the Sweet Pie Crust
with the sweetness from the berry saves 55 calories per serving.*

Lemonade Tart

I love this recipe for its simplicity. Lemons are one of the top foods to eat with miracle berries, and this recipe takes advantage of the fact that they taste like lemonade.

Ingredients

Flour, for rolling the dough

½ recipe Sweet Pie Crust (page 132)

5 large eggs

¾ cup freshly squeezed lemon juice

Grated zest of 3 lemons

1 cup agave nectar

Pinch of salt

12 tablespoons (1 ½ sticks) unsalted butter, cut into tablespoons

Directions

Preheat the oven to 350 degrees F.

On a lightly floured surface, roll out the dough to a circle of 12 inches in diameter. Place the dough in a 9-inch pie plate and gently tamp it down. Crimp the edge with your fingers or a fork. Prick the crust bottom with a fork, 2 inches apart. Line with parchment paper and fill with 2 cups dried beans, rice, or pie weights. Bake for 15 minutes. Remove the parchment and beans and bake another 5 minutes. Remove from the oven but leave the oven on. Let the crust cool while you make the filling.

In a medium saucepan, beat together the eggs, lemon juice, lemon zest, agave nectar, and salt. Cook over medium heat, stirring, until the filling coats the back of a spoon. Remove from the heat and add the butter a few pieces at a time, stirring until fully incorporated.

Pour into the crust. Bake for 15 minutes. Let cool before cutting.

When you are ready to eat, let the miracle berry tablet dissolve on your tongue and then enjoy the dish.

Replacing 1 ½ cups of sugar from the filling with 1 cup of agave nectar
and the sweetness from the berry, plus replacing ¼ cup of sugar from the Sweet Pie Crust with
1 tablespoon of agave nectar and the sweetness from the berry saves 29 calories per serving.

Key Lime Meringue Pie

MAKES ONE 9-INCH PIE (8 SERVINGS)

Here we use Key limes to provide the necessary sweetening and flavor for this classic. I love this with a nice glass of chenin blanc, which will taste like Sauternes (a fancy dessert wine) with the miracle berry. So you save 1,500 calories with the dessert, and that number is even higher when you pair it with chenin blanc instead of Sauternes.

Ingredients

2 tablespoons all-purpose flour, plus more for rolling the dough

½ recipe Sweet Pie Crust (page 132)

½ cup freshly squeezed Key lime juice

5 tablespoons honey

1 tablespoon cornstarch

3 large egg whites

¼ teaspoon cream of tartar

Pinch of salt

½ teaspoon pure vanilla extract

Lime slices, for garnish

Directions

Preheat the oven to 350 degrees F.

On a lightly floured surface, roll out the dough to a circle of 12 inches in diameter. Place the dough in a 9-inch pie plate and gently tamp it down. Crimp the edge with your fingers or a fork. Prick the crust bottom with a fork, 2 inches apart. Line with parchment paper and fill with 2 cups dried beans, rice, or pie weights. Bake for 15 minutes. Remove the parchment and beans and bake another 5 minutes. Let the crust cool while you make the filling.

In a small saucepan, combine the lime juice, 2 tablespoons of the honey, and the cornstarch. Cook over low heat until clear, stirring constantly. Remove from the heat.

In a large bowl, beat the egg whites, cream of tartar, and salt until foamy. Mix in the vanilla. Gradually add the remaining 3 tablespoons honey and 2 tablespoons flour, beating constantly, until soft peaks form. Gradually pour in lime juice mixture, beating until stiff. Pour into prepared piecrust and spread all the way to the edges. Garnish with lime slices.

When you are ready to eat, let the miracle berry tablet dissolve on your tongue and then enjoy the dish.

———————————

Replacing 2 cups of sugar from the filling with 5 tablespoons of honey and the sweetness from the berry, plus replacing 2 tablespoons of sugar from the Sweet Pie Crust with 1 tablespoon of agave nectar and the sweetness from the berry saves 157 calories per serving.

Pumpkin Pie

MAKES ONE 9-INCH PIE (8 SERVINGS)

Pumpkins are naturally sweet. However, they do need a slight boost of sweetness and here we add lemon juice to create just the right balance.

Ingredients

Flour, for rolling the dough

½ recipe Sweet Pie Crust
(page 132)

4 ¼-ounce packets unflavored
powdered gelatin

2 cups canned 100% pure pumpkin
puree

½ cup heavy cream

½ cup agave nectar

2 tablespoons freshly squeezed
lemon juice

½ teaspoon grated lemon zest

2 large eggs

1 large egg yolk

½ teaspoon salt

2 teaspoons ground cinnamon

¼ teaspoon ground nutmeg

¼ teaspoon ground cloves

¼ teaspoon ground cardamom

Directions

Preheat the oven to 350 degrees F.

On a lightly floured surface, roll out the dough to a circle of 12 inches in diameter. Place the dough in a 9-inch pie plate and gently tamp it down. Crimp the edge with your fingers or a fork. Prick the crust bottom with a fork, 2 inches apart. Line with parchment paper and fill with 2 cups dried beans, rice, or pie weights. Bake for 15 minutes. Remove from the oven but leave the oven on. Remove the parchment and beans. Let the crust cool while you make the filling.

In a medium bowl, sprinkle powdered gelatin into 2 tablespoons of water to bloom.

Mix the pumpkin, cream, agave nectar, lemon juice, lemon zest, eggs, and egg yolk until combined. Stir in the salt, cinnamon, nutmeg, cloves, cardamom, and gelatin. Pour into the prebaked crust and bake for 10 to 15 minutes until golden brown and set. Store in refrigerator covered in plastic.

When you are ready to eat, let the miracle berry tablet dissolve on your tongue and then enjoy the dish.

Replacing 2 cups of sugar from the filling with ½ cup of agave nectar and the sweetness from the berry, plus replacing ¼ cup of sugar from the Sweet Pie Crust with 1 tablespoon of agave nectar and the sweetness from the berry saves 137 calories per serving.

Mincemeat Pie

MAKES ONE 9-INCH PIE (8 SERVINGS)

When we first got this recipe correct, most people couldn't believe that pickle juice was added. Well, it works well and really provides a nice complexity to this classic.

Ingredients

Flour, for rolling the dough

½ recipe Sweet Pie Crust (page 132)

2 gelatin sheets or 1 scant teaspoon unflavored powdered gelatin

½ cup 80/20 ground beef

4 cups chopped peeled apples

1 ½ cups raisins

¼ cup Sweet Pickle Juice (page 261)

¼ cup pineapple juice

½ teaspoon salt

½ teaspoon ground cloves

1 teaspoon ground cinnamon

1 teaspoon ground nutmeg

½ cup agave nectar

Directions

Preheat the oven to 350 degrees F.

On a lightly floured surface, roll out the dough to a circle of 12 inches in diameter. Place the dough in a 9-inch pie plate and gently tamp it down. Crimp the edge with your fingers or a fork. Prick the crust bottom with a fork, 2 inches apart. Line with parchment paper and fill with 2 cups dried beans, rice, or pie weights. Bake for 15 minutes. Remove the parchment and beans and bake another 5 minutes. Remove from the oven but leave the oven on. Let the crust cool while you make the filling.

If using gelatin sheets, soak them in a small bowl of ice water for 3 minutes. Drain and squeeze out excess water. If using powdered gelatin, sprinkle on about 1 tablespoon water to bloom.

In a large skillet, brown the beef, breaking up any clumps thoroughly. Drain off any fat from the pan. Add the apples, raisins, pickle juice, pineapple juice, salt, cloves, cinnamon, nutmeg, and agave nectar. Bring to a boil, then turn down the heat to a simmer and cook for 15 minutes. Remove from heat and stir in the gelatin. Pour into the prebaked crust and bake for 10 minutes to heat through. Hold in refrigerator covered in plastic. Serve warm.

When you are ready to eat, let the miracle berry tablet dissolve on your tongue and then enjoy the dish.

———————————

Replacing 1 packed cup of brown sugar with ½ cup of agave nectar
and the sweetness from the berry, plus replacing ¼ cup of granulated sugar
from the Sweet Pie Crust with 1 tablespoon of agave nectar and the sweetness from the berry
saves 49 calories per serving.

Grasshopper Pie

MAKES ONE 9-INCH PIE (8 SERVINGS)

In this recipe, we gain sweetness from a blend of grapefruit and lime juices. The trick with this pie is to chill it before adding the hot fudge. The hot/cold combination is what really makes it special.

Ingredients

Flour, for rolling the dough

½ recipe Sweet Pie Crust (page 132)

½ cup half-and-half

½ cup skim milk

¼ cup fresh mint leaves

1 vanilla bean, split in half lengthwise

¼ cup agave nectar

Pinch of salt

2 large eggs

4 teaspoons cornstarch

6 tablespoons freshly squeezed lime juice

¼ cup freshly squeezed grapefruit juice

1 recipe Old-Fashioned Hot Fudge (page 251), for serving

Directions

Preheat the oven to 350 degrees F.

On a lightly floured surface, roll out the dough to a circle of 12 inches in diameter. Place the dough in a 9-inch pie plate and gently tamp it down. Crimp the edge with your fingers or a fork. Prick the crust bottom with a fork, 2 inches apart. Line with parchment paper and fill with 2 cups dried beans, rice, or pie weights. Bake for 15 minutes. Remove the parchment and beans and bake another 5 minutes. Remove from the oven but leave the oven on and turn down the oven temperature to 325 degrees F. Let the crust cool while you make the filling.

Combine the half-and-half, milk, and mint to a small saucepan. With a small knife, scrape the seeds out of each half of the vanilla bean and add to the cream mixture. (Save the pod for another use.) Cook over low heat for 10 minutes. Remove and discard the mint leaves. Stir in the agave nectar and salt, and slowly bring to a boil, stirring occasionally. When it comes to a boil, turn off the heat.

In a bowl, beat the eggs and cornstarch. Add about ½ cup of the hot liquid and whisk vigorously to combine. Whisk in a little more of the hot liquid. Gradually add the tempered eggs back to the hot liquid and whisk vigorously to combine. Over medium-low heat, slowly bring to a boil, scraping the bottom of the pan with a spatula. When the cream coats the back of the spatula, remove it from the heat. Gradually whisk in the lime and grapefruit juices, a couple tablespoons at a time, until smooth.

Pour into prebaked pie crust and bake for 35 minutes.

Cool on a wire rack. Refrigerate until firm. Serve with hot fudge.

When you are ready to eat, let the miracle berry tablet dissolve on your tongue and then enjoy the dish.

———————

Replacing 2 ¼ cups of sugar from the filling with ¼ cup of agave nectar and the sweetness from the berry, plus replacing 2 tablespoons of sugar in the Sweet Pie Crust with 1 tablespoon of agave nectar and the sweetness from the berry saves 190 calories per serving.

———————

Substituting our Old-Fashioned Hot Fudge for traditional hot fudge saves an additional 88 calories per serving, for a total of 278 calories saved per serving.

Raspberry Rhubarb Crostata

MAKES 8 SERVINGS

After eating a miracle berry, I could snack on raw rhubarb all day. It's sort of a bizarre exercise, as the texture reminds you of celery, but it tastes almost like pure sugarcane. In this recipe, we use rhubarb and lime juice to provide the sweetness. If you have an abundance of rhubarb in your garden, as I do, try juicing it and use to sweeten coffee or soda water.

Ingredients

2 cups unbleached all-purpose flour, plus more for rolling the dough

1 teaspoon salt

⅓ cup plus 1 tablespoon agave nectar

½ pound (2 sticks) cold butter, cut into tablespoons

2 large eggs

¼ cup cornstarch

3 tablespoons ice water

4 cups rhubarb slices, ½-inch wide

6 ounces fresh raspberries

2 cups freshly squeezed lime juice

1 tablespoon water

Directions

In a food processor, combine the flour and salt. Add 1 tablespoon of the agave nectar and the butter. Pulse until the texture is crumbly and the butter is reduced to pea-size pieces. Add 1 of the eggs and pulse until moist clumps form. Gather dough into a ball, handling it as little as possible. Place on a sheet of plastic wrap and pulling the sides up, flatten the dough into a disk. Wrap tightly and chill for at least 1 hour. (This dough can be made 2 days ahead and kept in the refrigerator.)

Mix the cornstarch with the ice water in a small bowl to make a slurry. Combine the rhubarb, raspberries, the remaining ⅓ cup agave nectar and the lime juice in a large saucepan. Cook over medium heat, stirring often, for about 4 minutes. Stir in the slurry and bring to a boil (the rhubarb will not be tender, and the slices will still be intact). Transfer to a bowl. Refrigerate until cool, about 30 minutes.

Preheat the oven to 400 degrees F.

On a lightly floured sheet of parchment paper, roll out the dough to a rough 12-inch round. Slide the parchment paper onto a large baking sheet. Beat the remaining egg with 1 tablespoon water to make an egg wash. Brush the crust with the egg wash. Mound the filling in the center of the crust. Gently spread it out, leaving a 1 ½-inch border around the outside. Fold the edges of the crust over the filling, overlapping as needed. Brush the top of the crust with egg wash. Bake until the crust is golden brown and and the filling bubbly, about 45 minutes. Let cool on the baking sheet on a wire rack before cutting into wedges. Store in refrigerator covered in plastic.

When you are ready to eat, let the miracle berry tablet dissolve on your tongue and then enjoy the dish.

Replacing 1 cup of sugar with about 6 tablespoons of agave nectar
and the sweetness from the berry saves 49 calories per serving.

Double Chocolate Peanut Butter Pie

Everyone loves chocolate and peanut butter desserts. At the restaurant, we call them "the crowd pleasers." The cream cheese, chunks of peanuts, chocolate, and that hint of salt make this a total winner.

Ingredients

8 ounces sugarless chocolate wafer cookies

1 cup unsweetened chocolate, chopped

4 tablespoons (½ stick) unsalted butter, cut into tablespoons

1 ½ cups cold heavy cream

8 ounces reduced-fat cream cheese, softened

1 cup sugar-free chunky peanut butter

½ cup agave nectar

2 teaspoons pure vanilla extract

¾ cup salted roasted peanuts, chopped

Pinch of kosher salt

Directions

Preheat the oven to 375 degrees F.

Grind the cookies into fine crumbs in a food processor, or by crushing with a rolling pin in a resealable plastic bag.

In a medium glass bowl, combine 4 ounces of the chocolate and the butter and microwave on high power in 20-second intervals until the chocolate is melted. Stir until smooth. Stir in the cookie crumbs. Press into the bottom of a 9-inch springform pan, going 1 ½ inches up the sides of the pan. Bake for 10 minutes. Let cool.

With an electric mixer, beat 1 cup of the cream to firm peaks. Transfer to another bowl. In the same mixer bowl, beat the cream cheese, peanut butter, agave nectar, and vanilla until well combined. Fold in one-third of the whipped cream. When combined, add the rest of the whipped cream and ½ cup of the chopped peanuts. Spoon into the baked crust and smooth the surface. Sprinkle with a pinch of kosher salt and refrigerate until firm, about 3 hours.

In a glass bowl, heat the remaining chocolate and ½ cup heavy cream in the microwave on high power in 20-second intervals until the chocolate is melted and the cream is hot. Stir until smooth. Let cool until barely warm, stirring occasionally.

Spread the chocolate cream over the chilled pie and refrigerate until firm, about 15 minutes. Sprinkle the remaining ¼ cup of chopped peanuts around the edge of the pie. Carefully run a thin knife around the edges of the pie crust to loosen it, then remove the springform ring. Cut the pie with a sharp knife, dipping it in hot water between cuts.

When you are ready to eat, let the miracle berry tablet dissolve on your tongue and then enjoy the dish.

Replacing 1 ½ cups of sugar with ½ cup of agave nectar
and the sweetness from the berry saves 84 calories per serving.

Pork Curry Dumplings with Sweet Ginger Garlic Sauce, page 55.

Banana Nut Muffins, page 40.

Blueberry Pancakes, page 18.

Champagne Fizz to "Lemon Drop," page 274.

Spicy Apricot Chicken Wings with Dipping Sauce, page 54.

Pumpkin Pie, page 143.

Chocolate Mousse, page 159.

Korean Beef with Quick Kim Chi and Spicy Sambal, page 102.

Peach Bread Pudding, page 173.

Jelly Donut Trifles, page 214.

Pad Thai, page 70.

Butternut Squash Soup, page 64.

Strawberry Shortcake, page 130.

Mojito, page 282.

Baked French Toast with Raspberry Syrup, page 24.

Cinnamon Spice Muffins, page 42.

Cranberry Orange Bread, page 44.

Lemon Poppy Seed Cake (page 110)
with Goat Cheese Frosting (page 269).

Pulled Pork Sandwiches, page 72.

Roast Chicken with 30-Minute Mole, page 77.

Orange Waffles, page 12.

Blueberry Muffins, page 38.

"Gin and Tonic" to Sloe Gin Screw, page 273.

Cheese Puffs, page 50.

Over-the-Top Lemon Layer Cake, page 112.

Molten Chocolate Cakes, page 124.

Strawberry Balsamic Ice Cream, Chocolate Ice Cream,
Vanilla Ice Cream with Old-Fashioned Hot Fudge, pages 236
232, 230, and 251.

Pear Tarte Tatin

MAKES ONE 10-INCH TART (6 SERVINGS)

Tarte Tatin is, hands down, my favorite dessert. The classic dessert is made with apples, but it's absolutely wonderful with pears and walnuts. In this recipe we add just a little sweetness with the lemon juice, as I prefer my desserts a little less sweet.

Ingredients

1 teaspoon ground cinnamon

6 tablespoons honey

6 firm, ripe medium Anjou pears, peeled, cut in half, and cored

3 tablespoons freshly squeezed lemon juice

1 sheet frozen puff pastry, thawed overnight in the refrigerator

Flour, for rolling the pastry

2 tablespoons water

Pinch of salt

4 tablespoons (½ stick) unsalted butter, cut into ¼-inch cubes

½ cup walnuts, coarsely chopped

Directions

Preheat the oven to 375 degrees F.

In a small bowl, combine the cinnamon and 2 tablespoons of the honey. Place the pear halves in a large bowl. Add the lemon juice and toss to coat. Add the cinnamon-honey and toss to coat.

Unfold the pastry sheet on a lightly floured surface. Invert a heavy 10-inch oven-safe skillet over the pastry sheet. Using the skillet as a template, trim the excess pastry to make a circle. Prick the pastry circle thoroughly with a fork. Transfer the pastry circle to a parchment paper–lined plate and refrigerate.

Heat the skillet over medium-high heat. Pour in the water, then the remaining ¼ cup honey. Cook for 7 minutes or until the honey is a deep amber. Do not stir.

Remove from the heat. Add the salt and butter. Carefully tilt the skillet so that the honey and butter swirl together until well blended. Let the mixture cool for 2 minutes.

Sprinkle the walnuts in the skillet. Drain the pears. Arrange 11 of the pear halves around the inside edge of the skillet, cut side up, overlapping slightly, with the stem end pointing toward the center. Place the remaining pear half, cut side up, in the gap in the center, trimming to fit if needed.

Cook the pears over medium heat for 10 minutes or until tender. Do not stir. Remove from the heat.

Invert the pastry circle over the pear halves, pressing down slightly and tucking the edge in around the inside of the skillet.

Transfer to the oven and bake for 40 minutes, or until the pastry is golden brown.

Let the tart cool in the skillet on a wire rack for 5 minutes. Carefully invert onto a serving plate. Serve immediately.

When you are ready to eat, let the miracle berry tablet dissolve on your tongue and then enjoy the dish.

Replacing ¾ cup of sugar with 6 tablespoons of honey
and the sweetness from the berry saves 32 calories per serving.

Pineapple Tarts

MAKES 4 TARTS (4 SERVINGS)

Pineapple is one of my favorite dessert ingredients. I love it in tarte Tatin, and it pairs great with cinnamon. In this recipe, lemon juice and acidity from the pineapples create the sweetness.

Ingredients

Canola oil spray

8 ounces reduced-fat cream cheese, softened

⅓ cup plus 1 tablespoon honey

1 tablespoon lemon juice

½ teaspoon ground cinnamon

4 frozen puff pastry shells, thawed overnight in the refrigerator

¼ cup whole milk

1 ½ cups slices fresh pineapple, in 1-inch pieces

Directions

Preheat the oven to 375 degrees F. Spray a baking sheet with canola oil.

Mix the cream cheese, ⅓ cup of the honey, and the cinnamon together in a bowl until thoroughly blended.

Place the puff pastry shells on the baking sheet. Mix the remaining 1 tablespoon honey with the lemon juice and brush each shell. Bake until the shells rise and turn golden brown, 10 to 15 minutes.

Remove the shells from oven (but leave the oven on) and use a fork to remove the caps (or thin top layer) from each puff pastry shell. This will come off easily and will be placed back on top later.

Spoon 2 tablespoons of the cream cheese filling into each shell. Top with pineapple slices. Place a puff pastry cap on top of each shell over the pineapple.

Return the filled pastry shells to oven, and bake until pastry caps are golden brown and the filling is warm, about 10 minutes more.

When you are ready to eat, let the miracle berry tablet dissolve on your tongue and then enjoy the dish.

Replacing ¾ cup of sugar with about 6 tablespoons of honey and the sweetness from the berry saves 43 calories per serving.

Blackberry Ricotta Tarts

MAKES 6 TARTS (6 SERVINGS)

When I was in culinary school and flat broke, I survived on pizza and microwaved cheese Danish. I know, it's shameful, but I thought they were even better than the ones we made in pastry class. Though my tastes have evolved considerably since those days, there is still nothing as satisfying to me as a warm Danish with oozing cheese. In this recipe, I've tried to make them as satisfying as the ones I remember. Quick tip: don't microwave these—eat them straight out of the oven.

Ingredients

½ cup low-fat ricotta cheese

Canola oil spray

5 sheets phyllo dough, thawed
  overnight in refrigerator

2 tablespoons unsalted butter
  or margarine, melted

4 ounces reduced-fat cream cheese
  (½ cup)

¼ cup honey

1 large egg

½ teaspoon grated orange zest

½ teaspoon pure vanilla extract

Pinch of ground nutmeg

2 cups fresh blackberries

1 tablespoon freshly squeezed
  lemon juice

Directions

Drain the ricotta in a fine-mesh strainer for 20 minutes.

Preheat the oven to 350 degrees F. Spray six 3-inch tart pans with removable bottoms with canola oil.

With the phyllo sheets in a stack, trace six squares (3 squares across and 2 squares vertical). Using a sharp knife, cut through all 5 sheets of dough along the traced lines. Line each tart pan with 5 sheets of dough, lightly brushing melted butter between each layer. Trim the edges of the dough flush with the top of the pans.

In a bowl, combine cream cheese, ricotta (discard the whey), honey, egg, orange zest, vanilla, and nutmeg. Beat with an electric mixer until smooth. Pour an equal amount of filling into each tart pan.

Bake until golden brown, about 25 minutes. Let the tarts cool for a minute or two. Arrange the berries on the top, and drizzle a little lemon juice over the fruit before serving.

When you are ready to eat, let the miracle berry tablet dissolve on your tongue and then enjoy the dish.

---

*Replacing ½ cup of sugar with ¼ cup of honey
and the sweetness from the berry saves 22 calories per serving.*

Chocolate Mousse

MAKES 2 ½ CUPS (8 SERVINGS, 5 TABLESPOONS EACH)

A good chocolate mousse recipe should really enhance the chocolate, so it is best to get the highest quality unsweetened chocolate you can find. For the sweetness, we use lemon juice; however, red wine or balsamic vinegar pairs nicely, as well.

Ingredients

6 ounces unsweetened chocolate, chopped

2 large pasteurized egg yolks

2 tablespoons agave nectar

2 tablespoons freshly squeezed lemon juice

2 tablespoons Kahlúa or other coffee liqueur

1 ½ cups cold heavy cream

Directions

Melt the chocolate in small bowl placed over a pan of simmering water. Do not let the bowl touch the water. Stir until smooth. Let cool slightly.

With an electric mixer, in a large bowl, beat the egg yolks and agave nectar until doubled in volume. Stir in the lemon juice and liqueur. Add the chocolate, beating vigorously.

In another large bowl, beat the cream until stiff peaks form. Carefully fold half of the whipped cream into the chocolate mixture, making sure not to deflate the cream. Fold the chocolate mixture back into the remaining whipped cream to gently incorporate.

Spoon into one large serving bowl or 8 small serving cups. Chill for at least 1 hour before serving.

When you are ready to eat, let the miracle berry tablet dissolve on your tongue and then enjoy the dish.

Replacing ¾ cup of sugar with 2 tablespoons of agave nectar and the sweetness from the berry saves 57 calories per serving.

Pots de Crème

MAKES 4 SERVINGS

In this recipe we use lime juice to sweeten the cream.

Ingredients

8 ounces chopped unsweetened chocolate

3 large eggs, at room temperature

2 teaspoons pure vanilla extract

¼ cup freshly squeezed lime juice

Pinch of salt

½ cup very hot brewed espresso or very strong coffee

Directions

In a blender, combine the chocolate, eggs, vanilla, lime juice, and salt. Cover the blender and turn on to high speed. While pureeing, carefully remove the circular disk from the blender lid and very slowly pour in the hot espresso. The espresso must be very hot for the final product to be the right consistency and texture.

Blend for a minute, scraping down the sides of the beaker as necessary, until mixture is smooth and fairly free of visible bits of chocolate. Pour into four serving cups and chill for 3 to 4 hours before serving.

When you are ready to eat, let the miracle berry tablet dissolve on your tongue and then enjoy the dish.

Replacing ⅓ cup of sugar with the sweetness from the berry saves 64 calories per serving.

Piña Colada Pudding

In this recipe, the acidity from the pineapple adds sweetness, as does lime juice.

Ingredients

1 pineapple, peeled, cored, and very coarsely chopped

2 quarts unsweetened coconut milk

½ cup agave nectar

½ teaspoon salt

½ cup cornstarch

⅓ cup freshly squeezed lime juice

¼ cup water

Directions

In a food processor, pulse the pineapple until coarsely chopped. In a large saucepan over medium heat, heat the coconut milk, agave nectar, and salt. Add the pineapple.

In a small bowl, whisk together the cornstarch, lime juice, and water to make a slurry. Whisk the slurry into the coconut milk mixture and cook until reduced and thickened, similar to the consistency of yogurt. Transfer to serving dishes and chill until firm.

When you are ready to eat, let the miracle berry tablet dissolve on your tongue and then enjoy the dish.

Replacing ¾ cup of sugar with ½ cup of agave nectar and the sweetness from the berry saves 12 calories per serving.

Butterscotch and Lime Custard

MAKES 8 SERVINGS

Here we re-create a butterscotch custard that is toasty and caramelized from the Scotch. The lime adds sweetness and also great contrast to the rich custard.

Ingredients

1 quart heavy cream

1 ½ cups whole milk

1 vanilla bean, split in half
   lengthwise

1 ½ cups plus 2 teaspoons
   Butterscotch Sauce (recipe follows)

2 large eggs

3 large egg yolks

½ cup cornstarch

¼ cup freshly squeezed lime juice

Directions

In a large saucepan, combine the cream and milk. With a small knife, scrape the seeds out of each half of the vanilla bean and add both seeds and pod to the cream mixture. Heat to just below boiling, about 180 degrees F. Stir in the butterscotch sauce and slowly bring to a boil. Turn off the heat and remove the vanilla bean pod. (Rinse off the pod and save for another use.)

In a medium bowl, combine the eggs, egg yolks, cornstarch, and lime juice. Add about ½ cup of the hot milk and whisk vigorously to combine. Whisk in a little more of the hot milk. Gradually add the tempered egg mixture back to the hot milk and whisk vigorously to combine. Slowly heat the custard over medium-low heat, stirring constantly. The custard is done when it coats the back of a spoon. Let cool slightly and pour into serving cups. Refrigerate to set before serving.

Replacing 1 ¾ cups of sugar in traditional butterscotch sauce with 1 cup of agave nectar and the sweetness from the berry in our Butterscotch Sauce saves 48 calories per serving.

Butterscotch Sauce

Ingredients

1 cup agave nectar

8 tablespoons (1 stick) butter, cut
into tablespoons
½ cup Scotch whiskey

Directions

Bring the agave nectar to a boil and cook on a low simmer for 10 minutes. Remove from the heat and add the butter, 1 tablespoon at a time, stirring to incorporate. Stir in the Scotch whiskey.

When you are ready to eat, let the miracle berry tablet dissolve on your tongue and then enjoy the dish.

Replacing 1 ¾ cups of sugar with 1 cup of agave nectar
and the sweetness from the berry saves 48 calories per serving.

Sticky Toffee Pudding

MAKES 8 SERVINGS

In England, in addition to being the general term for dessert, "pudding" means a dense, very moist cake; this dessert has a silky, melt-in-your-mouth texture that is unlike any cake you've had before. The sweetness in this dessert comes from lime juice. However, you can substitute half apple cider vinegar to provide an extra depth of flavor.

Ingredients

½ pound (2 sticks) unsalted butter, softened, plus more for the pan

1 cup self-rising cake flour (see note), plus more for the pan

1 cup pitted dates, finely chopped

1 ⅓ cups water

2 tablespoons agave nectar

1 large egg

Salt

3 cups freshly squeezed lime juice

Directions

Position a rack in the middle of the oven and preheat the oven to 350 degrees F. Butter and flour an 8-inch round cake pan.

In a small saucepan place the dates and 1 cup of the water. Cover and simmer for 5 minutes. Turn off the heat and let sit another 5 minutes, covered.

With an electric mixer, beat half of the butter with the agave nectar on medium-high speed until light and fluffy, about 4 minutes. Add the egg and beat until combined. Add the flour and ⅛ teaspoon salt and mix on low speed until just combined. Mix in the dates and lime juice.

Pour the batter into the pan and bake for 30 minutes, or until a toothpick comes out clean. Let cool in the pan on a wire rack.

While the cake is baking, melt the remaining stick of butter in a saucepan over medium heat. Stir in the remaining ⅓ cup water and a pinch of salt. Heat until boiling, stirring occasionally. Turn down the heat to a simmer and cook until the sauce is reduced to about ½ cup. Remove from heat but keep warm.

Poke cake with a chopstick or wooden spoon handle at 1-inch intervals. Gradually and evenly pour half of the warm sauce over the cake. Let stand until almost all of the sauce has been absorbed, about 20 minutes.

Run a thin knife around the edge of the pan. Invert a plate over the pan and, holding the pan and plate together, invert to drop the cake onto the plate. Pour any remaining warm sauce over the cake and serve immediately.

NOTE: If you don't have self-rising cake flour, you can make your own. For every cup of cake flour needed, place 2 tablespoons of cornstarch in a 1-cup measure, then fill the rest of the cup with all-purpose flour. Add 1 ½ teaspoons baking powder and ⅛ teaspoon salt. Sift the ingredients a few times to aerate the mixture.

When you are ready to eat, let the miracle berry tablet dissolve on your tongue and then enjoy the dish.

Replacing 1 cup of packed brown sugar and ¾ cup of granulated sugar with 2 tablespoons of agave nectar and the sweetness from the berry saves 161 calories per serving.

Thanksgiving Flummery with Cherry Compote

Much like a pudding, a flummery is a creamy, moist dessert that's not quite as firm as a cake. For this dessert, we are getting sweetness from the cherries and lime juice in the compote, as well as the lime juice in the flummery.

Flummery

¾ pound (3 sticks) unsalted butter, melted, plus more for the pan

4 ½ cups unbleached all-purpose flour, plus more for the pan

1 cup freshly squeezed lime juice

1 cup pitted prunes, quartered

⅔ cup agave nectar

4 large eggs, beaten

Grated zest of 6 limes

¼ teaspoon salt

1 tablespoon baking powder

2 teaspoons ground nutmeg

½ cup sliced almonds

½ cup shelled pistachios, chopped

Cherry Compote

1 ½ cups Bing cherries (frozen will work if it is not cherry season)

¼ cup water

½ cup freshly squeezed lime juice

1 cinnamon stick

¼ cup bourbon or whiskey

Directions

TO MAKE THE FLUMMERY: Preheat the oven to 325 degrees F. Butter and flour a 9-inch square cake pan.

In a saucepan, combine the lime juice and prunes. Cook over low heat for 10 minutes. Drain, reserving the lime juice.

In a large bowl, mix the butter and agave nectar. Add the eggs, lime zest, salt, and reserved lime juice and mix until combined. In a separate bowl, mix the flour, baking powder, nutmeg, prunes, almonds, and pistachios. Make a well in the flour and pour in the butter-egg mixture. Whisk until combined, but do not overmix. Pour into the pan and bake for 25 minutes or until a toothpick inserted in the center of the cake comes out clean. Cool in the pan on a wire rack.

TO MAKE THE COMPOTE: Pit the cherries and cut in half. Combine in a saucepan with the water, lime juice, and cinnamon over medium-high heat. Cook until the liquid is reduced by half. Remove from the heat and carefully add the bourbon. Return to low heat and cook until the liquid is again reduced by half, stirring occasionally.

Cut the flummery into 8 portions and serve with the warm compote.

When you are ready to eat, let the miracle berry tablet dissolve on your tongue and then enjoy the dish.

———————————

Replacing 1 ¼ cups of sugar with ⅔ cups of agave nectar
and the sweetness from the berry saves 40 calories per serving.

Orange Meringue Pudding

In this recipe we are using the acidity from the lemon, lime and orange juice to sweeten the pudding. If you want to make this a progressive dessert, try adding a pinch of saffron to the juices and allow it to simmer into the mixture.

Ingredients

2 tablespoons unsalted butter

Grated zest of 1 orange

1 cup freshly squeezed orange juice

½ cup freshly squeezed lime juice

½ cup freshly squeezed lemon juice

⅓ cup agave nectar

¼ cup cornstarch

¼ teaspoon salt

3 large eggs, separated

Directions

Preheat the oven to 425 degrees F.

In a medium saucepan, melt the butter over low heat. Whisk in the orange zest, orange, lime, and lemon juices, agave nectar, cornstarch, salt, and egg yolks. Turn up the heat to medium and bring to a simmer, whisking constantly until thickened, about 2 minutes. The trick to this step is to never stop whisking. Pour into four ramekins or oven-safe bowls.

In a large bowl, beat egg whites until stiff, glossy peaks form. Spread the egg whites over each pudding. Bake for 10 minutes, until the meringue is browned. Carefully allow ramekins to cool at room temperature and refrigerate for at least 1 hour before serving.

When you are ready to eat, let the miracle berry tablet dissolve on your tongue and then enjoy the dish.

Replacing ¾ cup of sugar with ⅓ cup of agave nectar
and the sweetness from the berry saves 64 calories per serving.

Vanilla and Thyme Panna Cotta with Balsamic Strawberries

MAKES 6 SERVINGS

This is a very simple and yet very flavorful dish. The better the balsamic vinegar, the more amazing this dish will taste. For an added depth of flavor, drizzle with just a touch of olive oil when serving.

Ingredients

One ¼-ounce packet unflavored powdered gelatin

½ cup cold water

Leaves from 2 sprigs thyme

1 vanilla bean, split in half lengthwise

2 cups heavy cream

¼ cup sour cream

1 pint strawberries, stemmed and cut in half lengthwise

¼ cup high-quality balsamic vinegar

Directions

In a medium bowl, sprinkle the gelatin into ¼ cup of the cold water and let sit for 5 to 10 minutes to bloom.

Bring the remaining ¼ cup water to a boil and add thyme leaves and vanilla bean. Let sit for a few minutes to infuse the flavor. Strain through a fine-mesh strainer into the gelatin and stir until the gelatin is completely dissolved, approximately 4 minutes

Whisk in the heavy cream and sour cream. Pour into six 8-ounce bowls and refrigerate for 3 hours or until set.

Toss the strawberries with the vinegar. Cover and refrigerate for 1 hour or as long as overnight.

To serve, gently warm the strawberries and vinegar and spoon on top of the panna cotta.

When you are ready to eat, let the miracle berry tablet dissolve on your tongue and then enjoy the dish.

———————

Replacing ⅔ cup of sugar with the sweetness from the berry saves 86 calories per serving.

Lime-Mint Flan

MAKES 4 FLANS (4 SERVINGS)

In this recipe the lemon, lime, and yogurt play off each other to create a very sweet and tangy flavor. It's a light way to end a meal that can be complemented with a glass of sauvignon blanc, which would take on a sweet riesling profile, but without the sugar.

Ingredients

½ cup water

Large bunch fresh mint,
    plus leaves for garnish

Juice of 3 limes

Grated zest of 2 limes

½ teaspoon unflavored powdered
    gelatin

1 ½ cups plain nonfat yogurt

2 tablespoons agave nectar

Canola oil spray

Lime zest strips

Directions

Place four 8-ounce ramekins in the refrigerator to chill.

In a small saucepan, bring the water and bunch of mint to a boil. Cover and turn down the heat to a simmer. Add gelatin and let infuse for 15 minutes. Strain into a large bowl and let cool to room temperature.

Stir the lime juice and zest into the mint-infused water. Let sit for 5 minutes to bloom, then mix very well. Mix together the yogurt with the agave nectar. Add to the gelatin mixture and mix well.

Remove the ramekins from the refrigerator and spray with canola oil. Fill with the flan mixture and refrigerate for at least 3 hours, until set.

To unmold, run a thin, sharp knife inside the edge of each ramekin. Bring 1 inch of water to a boil in a skillet. Place the ramekins in the water for 30 seconds, which will allow the flan to release from the ramekins easily. Invert the ramekins onto dessert plates. Serve the flans with fresh mint and strips of lime zest.

When you are ready to eat, let the miracle berry tablet dissolve on your tongue and then enjoy the dish.

Replacing 1 ¼ cups of sugar with 2 tablespoons of agave nectar and the sweetness from the berry saves 210 calories per serving.

Peach Bread Pudding

MAKES 6 TO 8 SERVINGS

When my daughter Grace says her favorite food is peaches, she means those juicy, plump, fragrant, end-of-the-summer peaches that drip down your chin. Unfortunately, the season for those peaches is very short. This recipe is a way to get around that—every peach will taste like the ones you find at the farmers' market.

Ingredients

Canola oil spray

2 or 3 large fresh peaches

1 cup whole milk

¼ cup honey

3 large eggs, lightly beaten

½ cup freshly squeezed orange juice

¼ cup freshly squeezed lemon juice

¼ cup freshly squeezed lime juice

¼ cup balsamic vinegar

4 tablespoons (½ stick) unsalted butter, melted

1 tablespoon pure vanilla extract

1 tablespoon ground cinnamon

1 teaspoon ground nutmeg

¼ teaspoon ground cloves

½ cup raisins (optional)

4 cups small cubes French bread, leaving the crust on.

Directions

Preheat an oven to 325 degrees F. Spray a 13 by 9-inch baking pan with canola oil. Bring a large pot of water to a boil. Fill a large bowl with ice and water.

Cut a small X in the bottom of each peach and place in the boiling water for 1 minute. Remove the peaches with a slotted spoon and submerge in the ice water. When cool, slip the skins off peaches. Cut the peaches in half, remove the pits, and cut the peaches into bite-size pieces.

In a separate large bowl, combine the milk, honey, and eggs. Stir in the orange, lemon, and lime juices, balsamic vinegar, butter, vanilla, cinnamon, nutmeg, and cloves. Stir in the peaches and raisins, if using, then the bread pieces, tossing to coat.

Pour into the baking pan and bake for 60 to 70 minutes, or until a knife inserted in the center of the pudding comes out clean.

When you are ready to eat, let the miracle berry tablet dissolve on your tongue and then enjoy the dish.

Replacing 2 ⅓ cups of sugar with ¼ cup of honey
and the sweetness from the berry saves 192 calories per serving.

Rice Pudding

SERVES 4

Warm, comforting, with subtle spice—everything you want in a classic fall dessert. We've chosen to use brown rice for health reasons, but you can use any short- or medium-grain rice, such as Arborio, for extra creaminess. For a modern twist, add a pinch of saffron to the cooking liquid.

Ingredients

1 ½ cups heavy cream

½ cup freshly squeezed orange juice

½ cup freshly squeezed lime juice

¼ cup plus 1 tablespoon freshly squeezed lemon juice

¼ teaspoon salt

½ cup short-grain brown rice

½ cup raisins (optional)

3 large egg yolks

¼ cup honey

½ teaspoon ground cinnamon, plus more for garnish

¼ teaspoon ground nutmeg

⅛ teaspoon ground cloves

1 tablespoon unsalted butter, softened

2 teaspoons pure vanilla extract

Directions

In a large saucepan, bring the cream, orange juice, lime juice, ¼ cup of the lemon juice, and the salt to a boil. Stir in the rice. Turn down the heat to low, cover, and cook until the liquid is completely absorbed, about 30 minutes. Fold in the raisins, if using, and continue cooking until the raisins plump, about 7 minutes more.

In a small bowl, whisk the egg yolks, honey, cinnamon, nutmeg, and cloves until combined. Slowly pour into the rice while stirring. Cook and stir until the pudding thickens, about 6 minutes. Remove from the heat and stir in the butter, vanilla, and the remaining 1 tablespoon lemon juice. Sprinkle with one last pinch of cinnamon. This can be served warm or chilled.

When you are ready to eat, let the miracle berry tablet dissolve on your tongue and then enjoy the dish.

Replacing ½ cup of sugar with ¼ cup of honey
and the sweetness from the berry saves 32 calories per serving.

Carrot Cake Whoopie Pies

MAKES 12 PIES (12 SERVINGS)

Whoopie pies are a huge hit for parties. Everyone loves individual (and portable) desserts. In this recipe, the cream cheese and lime juice add the sweetness, while the agave nectar provides the structure to give these a really special texture with a lot less guilt.

Ingredients

Canola oil spray

1 cup plus 2 tablespoons unbleached all-purpose flour

1 teaspoon ground cinnamon

½ teaspoon baking soda

½ teaspoon salt

8 tablespoons (1 stick) unsalted butter, softened

⅓ cup agave nectar

1 large egg

½ teaspoon pure vanilla extract

1 cup coarsely grated carrots

¾ cup walnuts, chopped

½ cup freshly squeezed lime juice

½ cup raisins

8 ounces reduced-fat cream cheese, softened

¼ cup honey

Directions

Position the racks in the upper and lower thirds of the oven. Preheat the oven to 375 degrees F. Spray two baking sheets with canola oil.

In a small bowl, whisk together the flour, cinnamon, baking soda, and salt. With an electric mixer, beat the butter, agave nectar, egg, and vanilla until pale and fluffy, about 2 minutes. Mix in the carrots, nuts, and raisins on low speed. Add the flour and mix until just combined.

Using 1 ½ tablespoons of batter per cookie, place cookies 2 inches apart on the baking sheets. Bake for 12 to 16 minutes, until lightly browned and springy to the touch. Switch the positions of baking sheets halfway through baking.

Cool the cookies on the baking sheets on wire racks for 1 minute, then transfer the cookies to racks to cool completely.

With an electric mixer, beat the cream cheese, lime juice and honey until smooth. Sandwich together the flat sides of two cookies with a generous tablespoon of cream cheese filling in between. Serve immediately or hold in refrigerator covered in plastic wrap.

When you are ready to eat, let the miracle berry tablet dissolve on your tongue and then enjoy the dish.

Replacing 3 ½ cups of sugar with ⅓ cup of agave nectar, ¼ cup of honey, and the sweetness from the berry saves 176 calories per serving.

Peanut Butter and Banana Whoopie Pies

MAKES 4 PIES (4 SERVINGS)

In this recipe, the sweetness is achieved with the lemon juice in the filling. These are great straight from the refrigerator, and even better frozen.

Peanut Butter Cookies

1 cup sugar-free peanut butter

¼ cup honey

1 cup vegetable shortening

2 large eggs

2 cups unbleached all-purpose flour

½ teaspoon salt

1 teaspoon baking powder

1 teaspoon baking soda

¼ cup finely chopped walnuts

Banana Cream Filling

½ cup cold heavy cream

½ tablespoon pure vanilla extract

½ teaspoon salt

¼ cup freshly squeezed lemon juice

½ cup mashed very ripe bananas

Directions

TO MAKE THE COOKIES: Preheat the oven to 350 degrees F.

In a large mixing bowl, beat the peanut butter, honey, and shortening. Add the eggs and mix well. In a separate bowl, mix the flour, salt, baking powder, baking soda, and walnuts. Add to the creamed mixture and mix until dough forms. Divide and roll the dough into 8 balls and place 3 inches apart on a baking sheet. Using a fork, gently flatten the dough, making a crisscross pattern. Bake for 8 to 9 minutes, until golden brown.

TO MAKE THE FILLING: With an electric mixer, whip the heavy cream, vanilla, salt, and lemon juice until stiff peaks form. Fold in the mashed bananas by hand so the cream doesn't deflate.

Sandwich the filling between pairs of cookies and refrigerate until firm, or freeze if desired.

When you are ready to eat, let the miracle berry tablet dissolve on your tongue and then enjoy the dish.

Replacing ⅔ cup of packed brown sugar and 1 ½ cups sugar with ¼ cup of honey and the sweetness from the berry saves 232 calories per serving.

Caramel Nut Bars

These bars have a luscious texture that is complemented by the crunch of pecans. When we tested this recipe, we found that champagne vinegar works well in place of the lime juice.

Cookie Base

Canola oil spray

2 cups unbleached all-purpose flour

1 teaspoon salt

1 tablespoon agave nectar

½ pound (2 sticks) cold unsalted butter, diced

1 large egg

Caramel Nut Topping

½ cup agave nectar

1 cup heavy cream

6 tablespoons unsalted butter, diced

¼ cup freshly squeezed lime juice

1 teaspoon pure vanilla extract

½ teaspoon salt

2 cups pecans, toasted and chopped

Directions

TO MAKE THE COOKIE BASE: Line a 13 by 9-inch baking pan with parchment paper, leaving a 2-inch overhang on the two short sides. Spray the parchment with canola oil.

In a food processor, combine the flour and salt. Add the agave nectar and butter, and pulse until the texture is crumbly and the butter is reduced to pea-size pieces. Add the egg and pulse until moist clumps form. Press the dough evenly onto the bottom of the baking pan, using plastic wrap on top to prevent the dough from sticking to your fingers. Chill until firm, about 20 minutes.

Position a rack in the middle of the oven and preheat the oven to 375 degrees F.

Remove plastic wrap and bake the cookie base until golden brown, about 30 minutes. Cool in pan on a wire rack for 20 minutes. (Leave the oven on.)

TO MAKE THE CARAMEL NUT TOPPING: In a large heavy saucepan, warm the agave nectar over medium heat, undisturbed, until it begins to bubble. Continue to cook, stirring occasionally with a fork. Tilt the pan and carefully pour in the cream. Cook with cream for approximately 2 minutes until the caramel is smooth and remove from the heat. Stir in the butter, lime juice, vanilla, salt and pecans. Immediately spread the topping over the crust and bake until bubbling, about 20 minutes.

Cool completely in the pan on a wire rack, about 2 hours, before cutting.

Holding the ends of the parchment paper lining, carefully lift the whole cookie out of the pan and place on a cutting board. Run a heavy knife under hot water for 10 seconds. Wipe dry and cut the cookie into bars. The bars can be stored in an airtight container for up to 3 days.

When you are ready to eat, let the miracle berry tablet dissolve on your tongue and then enjoy the dish.

Replacing ¾ cup of brown sugar and 2 ½ cups of granulated sugar
with 9 tablespoons of agave nectar and the sweetness from the berry saves 167 calories per serving.

Chocolate Coconut Oatmeal Bars

MAKES 24 BARS (12 SERVINGS)

In this recipe we use grapefruit to add a slight sweetness just to complement the coconut.

Ingredients

Canola oil spray

20 tablespoons (2 ½ sticks) unsalted butter, softened

¾ cup agave nectar

1 large egg

¼ cup freshly squeezed grapefruit juice

1 teaspoon pure vanilla extract

1 ½ cups unbleached all-purpose flour

1 teaspoon baking soda

1 teaspoon ground cinnamon

1 teaspoon salt

3 cups old-fashioned rolled oats

6 ounces chopped, unsweetened chocolate

2 ¼ cups unsweetened shredded coconut

Directions

Preheat the oven to 375 degrees F. Spray a 13 by 9-inch baking pan with canola oil.

With an electric mixer, in a large bowl beat the butter and agave nectar. Mix in the egg, grapefruit juice, and vanilla. In a separate bowl, combine the flour, baking soda, cinnamon, and salt. Fold into the butter mixture. Fold in the oats, chocolate, and coconut. Press into the pan and bake for 35 to 40 minutes.

Cool in pan on a wire rack before cutting into bars. The bars can be stored in an airtight container for up to 3 days.

When you are ready to eat, let the miracle berry tablet dissolve on your tongue and then enjoy the dish.

Replacing 1 ¼ cups of sugar with ¾ cup of agave nectar
and the sweetness from the berry saves 20 calories per serving.

Apple Cherry Oat Bars

MAKES 24 BARS (12 SERVINGS)

The acidity from the apples works well with the lime juice and the tartness from the cherries to produce a nice sweetness that ties these bars together.

Ingredients

½ pound (2 sticks) cold unsalted butter, diced, plus more for the pan

3 cups dried apples (about 7 ounces)

¾ cup dried cherries (about 4 ½ ounces)

1 ¾ cups freshly squeezed lime juice

1 teaspoon ground cinnamon

½ cup agave nectar

2 cups old-fashioned rolled oats

1 ½ cups unbleached all-purpose flour

½ teaspoon baking soda

½ teaspoon salt

Directions

Preheat the oven to 375 degrees. Butter a 13 by 9-inch baking pan.

Combine the apples, cherries, and lime juice in a large saucepan. Cover and simmer, stirring occasionally, for 5 minutes. When the fruits are softened and plump, drain them, reserving 2 tablespoons of the liquid. Let cool slightly.

Coarsely chop the fruit. Combine with ¼ teaspoon of the cinnamon and the reserved cooking liquid.

Whisk together agave nectar, the remaining ¾ teaspoon cinnamon, the oats, flour, baking soda, and salt in a large bowl. Cut in the butter with a pastry blender or fork until crumbs are the size of peas. Press 4 cups of the oat mixture into the bottom of the baking pan. Spread fruit filling on top, leaving a ¼-inch border on all sides. Sprinkle the remaining oat mixture on top. Bake until golden brown, about 35 minutes.

Cool in the pan on a wire rack. Cut into bars. The bars can be stored in an airtight container for up to 3 days.

When you are ready to eat, let the miracle berry tablet dissolve on your tongue and then enjoy the dish.

Replacing 1 packed cup of brown sugar with ½ cup of agave nectar and the sweetness from the berry saves 30 calories per serving.

Chocolate Cherry Coconut Bars

MAKES 8 BARS (8 SERVINGS)

For these bars we use lime juice and dried cherries to add the necessary sweetness with the miracle berry. The bitterness from the cocoa powder is slightly subdued and this allows for the chocolate flavor to come through in a more mellow tone.

Ingredients

Canola oil spray

1 ¼ cups dried cherries, coarsely chopped

20 tablespoons (2 ½ sticks) unsalted butter

¾ cup agave nectar

⅔ cup freshly squeezed lime juice

½ cup unsweetened Dutch-process cocoa powder

1 teaspoon kosher salt

1 cup unsweetened shredded coconut, lightly toasted

2 cups plus 2 ½ tablespoons all-purpose flour

1 large egg

2 ounces chopped, unsweetened chocolate

Directions

Preheat the oven to 325 degrees F. Line a 9-inch square baking pan with aluminum foil or parchment paper, allowing a 2-inch overhang on two sides. Spray with canola oil.

In a saucepan, bring the cherries, 2 tablespoons of the butter, the agave nectar, and the lime juice to a simmer over medium heat. Cook for 15 minutes, stirring occasionally, until almost all the liquid has been absorbed. Remove from the heat.

In a food processor, combine the cocoa powder, salt, coconut, and 2 cups of the flour. Dice the remaining butter, add, and process until the mixture resembles coarse meal. Press 3 cups into the bottom of prepared pan. Bake for 20 minutes, until just set. Remove from the oven but leave the oven on.

In an electric stand mixer fitted with a whisk, beat the egg on medium speed for

4 minutes. Fold in the cherry mixture, the remaining 2 ½ tablespoons flour, and the chocolate chunks. Spread evenly over the crust; sprinkle with the remaining crumbs. Bake for 50 minutes.

Cool in the pan on a wire rack. Holding the ends of the foil lining, carefully lift the whole cookie out of the pan and place on a cutting board. Cut into bars. The bars can be stored in an airtight container at room temperature up to 5 days.

When you are ready to eat, let the miracle berry tablet dissolve on your tongue and then enjoy the dish.

Replacing 1 ½ cups of sugar with ¾ cup of agave nectar
and the sweetness from the berry saves 54 calories per serving.

Cheesecake Bars

MAKES 24 BARS (12 SERVINGS)

Cream cheese is perhaps the most natural fit for miracle berries, which give it a flavor similar to cheesecake without any added sugar. With lime juice providing a flavor boost, these bars have the most wonderful cheesecake mouthfeel and flavor.

Ingredients

2 cups unbleached all-purpose flour

1 teaspoon salt

½ pound (2 sticks) cold unsalted butter, diced

1 tablespoon plus ½ cup agave nectar

2 tablespoons freshly squeezed lime juice

4 large eggs

16 ounces reduced-fat cream cheese, softened

½ cup grated lime zest

1 teaspoon vanilla or almond extract

1 cup fresh berries, such as raspberries or strawberries, or cherries, for serving

Mint leaves, for serving

Directions

Preheat the oven to 350 degrees F.

In a food processor, combine the flour and salt. Add the butter and pulse until it forms a coarse meal. Add 1 tablespoon of the agave nectar, the lime juice, and 1 of the eggs, and pulse until the dough comes together. Press into an ungreased 13 by 9-inch baking pan. Bake for 12 to 15 minutes, until lightly browned. Remove from the oven but leave the oven on.

With an electric mixer, beat the cream cheese, the remaining ½ cup agave nectar, and the lime zest until smooth. Add the remaining eggs and the vanilla and beat for 5 minutes, until stiff peaks are formed. Pour over the crust. Bake for 20 minutes.

Cool completely in the pan on a wire rack before slicing. Garnish with berries and mint.

When you are ready to eat, let the miracle berry tablet dissolve on your tongue and then enjoy the dish.

———————————

Replacing 1 ¼ cups of sugar with 9 tablespoons of agave nectar
and the sweetness from the berry saves 35 calories per serving.

Date Bars

The natural sweetness of dates is enhanced by the lemon juice in this recipe. This enhances the unsweetened applesauce nicely.

Ingredients

2 ¼ cups pitted dates

½ cup apple cider

¼ cup freshly squeezed lemon juice

1 ¼ cups whole-wheat flour

1 cup unbleached all-purpose flour, plus more for rolling the dough

¼ cup Bob's Red Mill wheat bran (if not available at your local grocer, you can find this online)

¼ teaspoon kosher salt

2 teaspoons baking soda

⅓ cup agave nectar

1 teaspoon grated lemon zest

10 tablespoons (1 ¼ sticks) unsalted butter, softened

1 large egg

¼ cup smooth unsweetened applesauce

Directions

In a saucepan, bring the dates and cider to a boil over medium-high heat. Turn down the heat and simmer until the dates are soft and almost all liquid has been reduced, about 10 minutes. Let cool completely. Transfer to a food processor with the lemon juice. Puree until smooth.

Whisk together the whole-wheat and all-purpose flours, the wheat bran, salt, and baking soda in a medium bowl. In an electric stand mixer fitted with a paddle, combine agave nectar and lemon zest. Mix on medium speed for 30 seconds. Add the butter and beat until combined, about 1 minute. Add the egg and mix until fluffy. Add the flour mixture one-third at a time, alternating with the applesauce. Mix until just combined. Divide the dough in half. Shape each half into a rectangle and wrap in plastic. Refrigerate until firm, about 2 hours.

Roll out half of the dough between two lightly floured sheets of parchment paper to form a 12 by 10-inch rectangle. Remove the top piece of parchment. Trim the dough to an 11 by 9-inch rectangle and transfer, still on the parchment, to a baking sheet. Cut the rectangle in half lengthwise. Spread a heaping cup of filling down each length, ¼-inch from one long side. Fold the dough over the filling and pinch to seal, using fork if desired. Repeat with the remaining dough and filling. Refrigerate until firm, about 20 minutes.

While the strips are firming up, preheat the oven to 375 degrees F.

Bake until golden brown, about 20 minutes. Cool the strips on the baking sheets on wire racks for 5 minutes. Cut each strip into 6 bars. Transfer carefully the bars to wire racks to cool completely. The bars can be stored in an airtight container for up to 3 days.

When you are ready to eat, let the miracle berry tablet dissolve on your tongue and then enjoy the dish.

———————————

*Replacing 1 ½ packed cups of brown sugar with 1/3 cup of agave nectar
and the sweetness from the berry saves 78 calories per serving.*

Chewy Amaretti Cookies

MAKES 24 COOKIES (12 SERVINGS)

I love amaretti cookies. This recipe is amazingly simple to make and uses lime juice to produce an intensely sweet cookie.

Ingredients

¾ cup Almond Paste (page 258)

½ cup agave nectar

¾ cup freshly squeezed lemon juice

2 large egg whites,
at room temperature

Directions

Position the racks in the upper and lower thirds of the oven and preheat the oven to 300 degrees F. Line two large baking sheets with parchment paper.

In a food processor, pulse the almond paste, agave nectar, and lemon juice until broken up. Add the egg whites and pulse until smooth. Transfer to a pastry bag with a plain tip or a heavy-duty resealable plastic bag. If using a plastic bag, push the dough to one corner and snip off a small bit of the corner. Pipe the dough into ¾-inch rounds, ⅓-inch high, about 1 inch apart on the pans.

Dip a fingertip in water and gently pat down any peaks on the cookies. Bake for 15 to 18 minutes, until golden and puffed, rotating and switching position of pans halfway through. Cool cookies in pans on wire racks and store in refrigerator covered in plastic.

When you are ready to eat, let the miracle berry tablet dissolve on your tongue and then enjoy the dish.

Replacing 1 ¼ cups of sugar with the sweetness from the berry saves 41 calories per serving.

Fudge-Striped Spice Cookies

MAKES 24 COOKIES (12 SERVINGS)

For these cookies we have omitted some whole milk and replaced it with lime juice. The richness from the chocolate makes up for this and the sweetness from the lime juice makes the chocolate seem sweeter than it is.

Ingredients

Canola oil spray

¾ cup pecans

8 tablespoons (1 stick) unsalted butter

½ cup agave nectar

½ cup freshly squeezed lime juice

1 cup unbleached all-purpose flour

¼ teaspoon ground nutmeg

¼ teaspoon ground mace

½ teaspoon ground cinnamon

1 cup chopped, unsweetened chocolate

Directions

Preheat the oven to 350 degrees F. Spray two baking sheets with canola oil.

In a food processor, grind pecans until they resemble fine crumbs.

In a small saucepan, melt the butter. Stir in the agave nectar and lime juice and bring to boil. Turn off the heat and stir in the ground pecans, flour, nutmeg, mace, and cinnamon. Mix well.

Using 1 teaspoon of dough for each cookie, place cookies on the baking sheets, spacing them 2 inches apart. Bake for 5 to 8 minutes, or until brown around the edges and lacey in appearance.

Cool on the baking sheets for 5 minutes, then transfer to wire racks to cool completely.

Place the chocolate pieces in a bowl over a pan of simmering water, making sure the bottom of the bowl does not touch the water. Stir until the chocolate is melted and smooth. Using a spoon, drizzle chocolate stripes across each cookie and serve immediately or store in refrigerator covered with plastic.

When you are ready to eat, let the miracle berry tablet dissolve on your tongue and then enjoy the dish.

---

*Replacing 1 ½ cups of sugar with ½ cup of agave nectar
and the sweetness from the berry saves 56 calories per serving.*

Lemon-Thyme Cookies

MAKES 36 COOKIES (18 SERVINGS)

Typically, lemon and thyme are combined in salads and cold appetizers. But why not a cookie? These are wonderfully complex, and with the goat cheese, they simply burst with flavor. The goat cheese adds sweetness, as does the lemon juice.

Cookies

2 ½ cups unbleached all-purpose flour

1 teaspoon baking powder

1 teaspoon salt

1 tablespoon fresh thyme leaves

8 tablespoons (1 stick) unsalted butter, softened

½ cup agave nectar

2 large eggs

2 cups fresh goat cheese (8 ounces)

5 tablespoons freshly squeezed lemon juice

Grated zest of 3 lemons

Glaze

1 cup freshly squeezed lemon juice

¼ cup agave nectar

Directions

TO MAKE THE COOKIES: Preheat the oven to 375 degrees F. Line two baking sheets with parchment paper.

In a medium bowl combine the flour, baking powder, salt, and thyme. With an electric mixer, in another bowl, beat the butter and agave nectar for 3 minutes, until fully mixed together. Add the eggs one at a time, beating each until incorporated. Add the goat cheese, lemon juice, and lemon zest. Beat to combine. Stir in the flour.

Using 2 tablespoons of dough for each cookie, place cookies on the baking sheets, spacing 2 inches apart. Bake for 15 minutes, or until slightly golden at the edges.

Cool on the baking sheets for 20 minutes.

TO MAKE THE GLAZE: While the cookies are cooling, in a medium saucepan, bring the lemon juice and agave nectar to a boil. Lower the heat to a simmer and cook for 15 minutes, or until thickened.

Drizzle the cookies with the glaze and serve immediately or store in refrigerator covered with plastic.

When you are ready to eat, let the miracle berry tablet dissolve on your tongue and then enjoy the dish.

_____

Replacing 2 ¼ cups of sugar with ½ cup of agave nectar
and the sweetness from the berry saves 70 calories per serving.

Cornmeal Cookies

For these cornmeal cookies, I use Meyer lemon juice. It is slightly less acidic than regular lemons, which means just slightly less sweet with the miracle berry. These make great ice cream sandwiches, and are fabulous dipped in a glass of milk.

Cornmeal Cookies

4 tablespoons (½ stick) unsalted butter, melted

¼ cup agave nectar

Grated zest of 3 large limes

1 large egg, at room temperature

3 tablespoons Meyer lemon juice

½ teaspoon pure vanilla extract

1 ½ cups rice flour, plus more for kneading

½ cup finely ground yellow cornmeal

½ teaspoon baking powder

¼ teaspoon fine sea salt

Icing

⅓ cup agave nectar

3 tablespoons freshly squeezed Meyer lemon juice

Grated zest of 2 large limes

1 tablespoon unbleached all-purpose flour

Directions

TO MAKE THE COOKIES: In a large bowl, combine the butter, agave nectar, and lime zest. Add the egg, lemon juice, and vanilla and whisk until smooth. Add the rice flour, cornmeal, baking powder, and salt. Stir until the dough holds together. Turn out the dough onto a lightly floured surface and knead for 20 seconds. Form the dough into a ball, wrap in plastic, and refrigerate for 20 minutes.

Position a rack in the middle of the oven and preheat the oven to 350 degrees F. Line a baking sheet with parchment paper.

On a lightly floured work surface, roll the dough ¼-inch thick. Using a 3-inch round cookie cutter or glass, cut 12 cookies. Carefully transfer to the baking sheet. Bake for 15 to 20 minutes, until lightly golden around the edges.

Cool on the pan for 10 minutes, then transfer to a wire rack to cool completely, about 15 minutes.

TO MAKE THE ICING: In a medium bowl, whisk the agave nectar, lemon juice, lime zest, and flour until smooth. Spread about 1 teaspoon of the glaze onto each cookie, leaving a ¼-inch border around the edge. Allow the glaze to harden for about 45 minutes before serving.

When you are ready to eat, let the miracle berry tablet dissolve on your tongue and then enjoy the dish.

Replacing 2 cups of sugar with ¼ cup of agave nectar in the dough and ⅓ cup of agave nectar in the icing, plus the sweetness from the berry saves 82 calories per serving.

Iced Pumpkin Cookies

MAKES 24 COOKIES (12 SERVINGS)

These are interesting, because the icing actually does not taste all that sweet. It's only after a couple bites that you realize the sweetness comes from the lime juice in the cookies.

Pumpkin Cookies

½ pound (2 sticks) unsalted butter, melted

½ cup agave nectar

1 cup canned 100% pure pumpkin puree

½ cup freshly squeezed lime juice

1 large egg

1 teaspoon pure vanilla extract

2 cups unbleached all-purpose flour

1 teaspoon baking powder

½ teaspoon baking soda

½ teaspoon salt

1 teaspoon ground cinnamon

½ teaspoon ground nutmeg

1 cup walnuts, coarsely chopped

1 cup raisins

Icing

4 tablespoons (½ stick) unsalted butter, melted

1 cup agave nectar

1 teaspoon pure vanilla extract

3 tablespoons heavy cream

Directions

TO MAKE THE COOKIES: Preheat the oven to 350 degrees F. Line two baking sheets with parchment paper.

In a large bowl, combine the butter and agave nectar. Add the pumpkin, lime juice, egg, and vanilla and mix well. In a separate bowl, combine the flour, baking powder, baking soda, salt, cinnamon, and nutmeg. Stir into the butter until well blended. Fold in the walnuts and raisins.

Using 2 tablespoons of dough for each cookie, place cookies onto the baking sheets, spacing them 2 inches apart. Bake for 15 minutes, or until golden.

Cool on the baking sheets for 5 minutes. Transfer to wire racks to cool completely.

TO MAKE THE ICING: With an electric mixer, beat the butter and agave nectar until creamy. Add the vanilla and cream and beat until smooth. Spread the icing on the cooled cookies and serve immediately or store in refrigerator covered in plastic.

When you are ready to eat, let the miracle berry tablet dissolve on your tongue and then enjoy the dish.

---

*Replacing 2 ⅓ cups of sugar with ½ cup of agave nectar in the dough
and 1 cup of agave nectar in the icing, plus the sweetness from the berry
saves 30 calories per serving.*

Italian Fig Cookies

MAKES 48 COOKIES (24 SERVINGS)

These are a little more complex to prepare than a standard cookie dough. However, the payoff is worth it. Many layers of flavors come through, and the sweetness comes from the lemon juice with the miracle berry.

Filling

2 cups dried figs, hard tips discarded

1 ½ cups dried dates, chopped

1 cup raisins

¾ cup almonds, toasted and chopped

¾ cup walnuts, toasted and chopped

¼ cup freshly squeezed lemon juice

¼ cup agave nectar

¼ cup brandy

3 teaspoons grated orange zest

4 teaspoons grated lemon zest

1 teaspoon ground cinnamon

½ teaspoon ground nutmeg

¼ teaspoon ground cloves

Dough

4 cups unbleached all-purpose flour, plus more for kneading

1 tablespoon plus 1 teaspoon baking powder

½ teaspoon salt

1 tablespoon grated lime zest

½ cup agave nectar

½ pound (2 sticks) cold unsalted butter, diced

1 large egg

½ cup skim milk

1 tablespoon pure vanilla extract

Canola oil spray

1 large egg white

1 tablespoon water

Directions

TO MAKE THE FILLING: In a food processor, finely chop the figs, dates, and raisins. Transfer to a bowl and stir in the almonds, walnuts, lemon juice, agave nectar, brandy, orange zest, lemon zest, cinnamon, nutmeg, and cloves. Cover and refrigerate for at least 8 hours.

TO MAKE THE DOUGH: In a food processor, combine the flour, baking powder, salt, lime zest, and agave nectar. Add the butter and pulse until the mixture resembles coarse meal. In a small bowl, beat the egg, milk, and vanilla. Add to the flour and pulse until a rough dough forms. Turn out the dough onto a lightly floured surface and knead until smooth, about 5 minutes. Cut the dough into four pieces, wrap in plastic, and refrigerate for 45 minutes.

Preheat the oven to 375 degrees F. Lightly spray two large baking sheets with canola oil.

On a lightly floured surface, working with one piece at a time, roll the dough into a 12-inch square. Cut the dough into 4 by 3-inch rectangles. Spoon 2 tablespoons of the filling down the center of each rectangle the long way. Fold the long sides of each rectangle inward to the center to enclose the filling. Pinch the ends to seal. Turn the cookies seam side down and press gently to flatten the seams. With a floured knife, cut the logs crosswise into 1 ½-inch-wide slices and arrange ½ inch apart on the baking sheets. Repeat with the remaining dough and filling.

Lightly beat the egg white and water to make an egg wash. Brush the tops with the egg wash and bake for 20 minutes, until golden brown. Serve immediately or refrigerate and cover with plastic wrap.

When you are ready to eat, let the miracle berry tablet dissolve on your tongue and then enjoy the dish.

Replacing 2 cups of sugar with ¼ cup of agave nectar in the dough and ½ cup of agave nectar in the filling, plus the sweetness from the berry saves 35 calories per serving.

Jam Thumbprint Cookies

MAKES 32 COOKIES (16 SERVINGS)

These cookies get a very pleasant tropical fruit quality from the mango jam and coconut flakes. The lime juice enhances this effect, as well as being the primary sweetener.

Ingredients

1 ¼ pounds (5 sticks) unsalted
    butter, melted

¼ cup agave nectar

¼ cup freshly squeezed lime juice

1 teaspoon pure vanilla extract

3 ½ cups unbleached all-purpose flour,
    plus more for shaping the dough

¼ teaspoon kosher salt

1 large egg

1 tablespoon water

2 ½ cups unsweetened shredded
    coconut

¼ cup Mango Jam (page 255)

Directions

In an electric stand mixer fitted with a paddle, mix together the butter, agave nectar, and lime juice until combined. Add the vanilla. In a separate bowl, sift together the flour and salt. With the mixer on low speed, add the flour to the butter and mix until the dough starts to come together. Turn out dough onto on a floured work surface and roll into a flat disk. Wrap in plastic and chill for 30 minutes.

Preheat the oven to 350 degrees F.

In a shallow bowl, beat together the egg and water. Place the coconut in another shallow bowl. Roll the dough into 1 ¼-inch balls. Dip each ball in the egg, roll in the coconut, and place on an ungreased baking sheet. Space the cookies so they do not touch. Make a light indentation in the top of each cookie with thumb. Spoon ¼ teaspoon jam into each indentation. Bake for 20 to 25 minutes, until the coconut is a golden brown. Cool on baking sheets, then transfer to a wire rack.

When you are ready to eat, let the miracle berry tablet dissolve on your tongue and then enjoy the dish.

—————

Replacing 2 ¼ cups of sugar with ¼ cup of agave nectar
and the sweetness from the berry in the cookies and replacing the tablespoon of sugar
from the Mango Jam with the sweetness from the berry saves 99 calories per serving.

Banana Almond Cookies

MAKES 36 COOKIES (18 SERVINGS)

In this recipe, the lime juice provides the sweetness with the miracle berry, while it also adds a slight citrusy note that complements the banana.

Ingredients

Softened, unsalted butter

2 ¼ cups blanched whole almonds

½ cup agave nectar

½ teaspoon almond extract

3 tablespoons freshly squeezed lime juice

1 large ripe banana, chopped

1 tablespoon grated lime zest

1 large egg white, lightly beaten

Directions

Line two baking sheets with parchment paper and lightly butter.

In a food processor, grind the almonds into coarse powder. Add the agave nectar and pulse until smooth. Transfer to an electric stand mixer fitted with a paddle. Add the almond extract, lime juice, banana, lime zest, and egg white. Mix on low speed until a sticky, heavy paste forms. Transfer to a pastry bag with a plain tip or a large heavy-duty resealable plastic bag. If using a plastic bag, push the dough to one corner and snip off a small bit of the corner.

Pipe strips of dough 3 by ¾ inches onto the parchment about ½ inch apart. Chill, uncovered, overnight (8 to 12 hours).

Position the racks in the upper and lower thirds of the oven and preheat the oven to 300 degrees F.

Bake the cookies for 20 minutes, rotating the sheets and switching positions half-way through baking. Remove the cookies from the oven but leave the oven on.

Cool the cookies on the baking sheets on wire racks for 10 minutes. Return the cookies to the oven and bake 15 minutes more.

Cool completely on the baking sheets on wire racks. Peel the cookies from the paper.

When you are ready to eat, let the miracle berry tablet dissolve on your tongue and then enjoy the dish.

————————————

Replacing 1 ½ cups of sugar with ½ cup of agave nectar and the sweetness from the berry saves 38 calories per serving.

Pistachio Cookies

MAKES 36 COOKIES (18 SERVINGS)

Pistachio cookies are perhaps my favorite kind of cookie. I love the complex flavor of pistachios, and here they are complemented by the lime zest, almond extract, and lime juice for sweetness.

Ingredients

1 cup agave nectar

½ cup grated lime zest (6 to 8 limes)

4 ½ cups unbleached all-purpose flour

1 ½ teaspoons baking powder

1 ½ teaspoons salt

1 pound (4 sticks) cold unsalted butter, diced

1 ⅓ cups chopped shelled pistachios

4 large egg yolks

2 teaspoons pure vanilla extract

⅛ teaspoon almond extract

1 ¾ cups freshly squeezed lime juice

Directions

In a small bowl, combine the agave nectar and ¼ cup lime zest. In a food processor, combine the flour, baking powder, and salt. Add the agave-zest mixture. Pulse to combine. Add the butter and half of the pistachios and process for 10 seconds. Add remaining pistachios and process for 5 seconds. In another bowl, whisk together the egg yolks, vanilla, almond extract, and lime juice. Pour into the food processor and process until a dough forms. Wrap in plastic and refrigerate until cold, but not solid, about 30 minutes.

Preheat the oven to 350 degrees F. Line two baking sheets with parchment paper.

Spread remaining ¼ cup of lime zest onto a plate. Using 1 tablespoon of dough per cookie, roll into balls and dip the balls into lime zest, so the top is covered. Place the balls zest side up on the baking sheet 3 inches apart. Using the bottom of a small glass wrapped in plastic wrap, gently flatten the cookies to ¼-inch thick.

Bake for 15 minutes, until slightly browned. Transfer the sheet of parchment paper to a wire rack to cool. Serve immediately or refrigerate covered with plastic.

When you are ready to eat, let the miracle berry tablet dissolve on your tongue and then enjoy the dish.

———————

Replacing 3 cups of sugar with 1 cup of agave nectar and the sweetness from the berry saves 75 calories per serving.

Fluffy Oatmeal Raisin Cookies

MAKES 12 COOKIES (12 SERVINGS)

These cookies are sweetened with the addition of lime juice. However, you can use apple cider vinegar to give them a slightly savory edge, which can be nice if you use them for ice cream sandwiches.

Ingredients

Canola oil spray

½ pound (2 sticks) unsalted butter, softened

¾ cup agave nectar

1 large egg

¼ cup freshly squeezed lime juice

2 cups unbleached all-purpose flour

½ teaspoon baking soda

½ teaspoon salt

1 tablespoon grated lime zest

½ teaspoon ground cinnamon

¼ teaspoon ground nutmeg

2 ½ cups quick-cooking rolled oats

½ cup raisins

Directions

Preheat the oven to 350 degrees F. Spray two baking sheets with canola oil.

With an electric mixer, beat the butter and agave nectar until creamy. Add the egg and lime juice and beat until combined. In a separate bowl, combine the flour, baking soda, salt, lime zest, cinnamon, and nutmeg. Gradually add to the butter mixture, beating until incorporated. Stir in the oats and raisins. Scoop six 1 ½-inch balls onto each baking sheet. Bake for 10 to 13 minutes, until lightly browned.

Cool the cookies for 2 minutes on the baking sheets, then transfer to wire racks to cool completely.

When you are ready to eat, let the miracle berry tablet dissolve on your tongue and then enjoy the dish.

Replacing 1 ½ cups of packed brown sugar with ¾ cup of agave nectar and the sweetness from the berry saves 44 calories per serving.

Chocolate Espresso Cookies

MAKES 12 COOKIES (12 SERVINGS)

Sour cream and lime juice sweeten and enhance the espresso and chocolate flavors in these cookies.

Ingredients

2 tablespoons unsalted butter, melted

6 ounces unsweetened chocolate, chopped into ½-inch pieces

½ cup finely ground espresso beans

1 cup unbleached all-purpose flour

2 tablespoons unsweetened Dutch-process cocoa powder

1 teaspoon baking powder

1 tablespoon grated lime zest

¼ teaspoon fine sea salt

¼ cup agave nectar

¼ cup low-fat sour cream

2 large eggs, at room temperature

3 tablespoons freshly squeezed lime juice

1 teaspoon pure vanilla extract

Directions

Position a rack in the middle of the oven and preheat the oven to 300 degrees F. Line two baking sheets with parchment paper or silicone mats.

Place the butter and chocolate in a small bowl placed over a saucepan of barely simmering water. Do not let the bowl touch the water. Stir occasionally until the chocolate has melted and the mixture is smooth.

In a separate bowl, whisk together the espresso, flour, cocoa powder, baking powder, lime zest, and salt. In another bowl, whisk together the agave nectar, sour cream, eggs, lime juice, and vanilla. Gradually fold in the espresso-flour mixture. Stir until thick and smooth. Fold in the melted chocolate.

Using an ice cream scoop, scoop ¼ cup of batter for each cookie onto the baking sheets. Bake for 18 to 20 minutes, until slightly puffed and the tops begin to crack.

Cool completely on the baking sheets on wire racks.

When you are ready to eat, let the miracle berry tablet dissolve on your tongue and then enjoy the dish.

———————————————

Replacing 1 ¾ cups sugar with ¼ cup of agave nectar
and the sweetness from the berry saves 92 calories per serving.

Chocolate-Covered Truffles

MAKES 30 TRUFFLES (15 SERVINGS)

This recipe uses lime juice for sweetening and brandy for an extra kick. Tequila would also be delicious, bringing in an almost margarita-like flavor.

Ingredients

18 ounces unsweetened chocolate, finely chopped

3 tablespoons unsalted butter

½ cup heavy cream

1 tablespoon agave nectar

¼ cup brandy

½ cup freshly squeezed lime juice

Optional Toppings

½ cup unsweetened cocoa powder

½ cup blanched almonds, finely chopped

½ cup toasted unsweetened coconut mixed with 1 tablespoon ground cinnamon

Directions

Line a baking sheet with parchment paper.

Place 10 ounces of the chocolate and the butter in a microwave-safe bowl. Microwave for 30 seconds on half power. Remove and stir. Repeat once more.

Heat the cream and agave nectar in a small saucepan over medium heat until simmering. Remove from the heat and pour over the melted chocolate; let stand for 2 minutes. Using a rubber spatula, stir gently, starting in the middle of bowl and working in concentric circles until all chocolate is melted and the mixture is smooth and creamy. Gently stir in the brandy and lime juice.

Pour into an 8-inch square glass baking dish and refrigerate for 1 hour. Using a melon baller or small spoon, place scoops of chocolate on the baking sheet. Refrigerate for 30 minutes.

Place the cocoa powder, almonds, and toasted coconut in separate bowls, if using.

Remove the truffles from the refrigerator and shape into balls. (If desired, to keep your hands clean wear disposable gloves.) Return them to the baking sheet, or put on a clean sheet of parchment paper.

Place the remaining 8 ounces chocolate in a microwave-safe bowl and microwave for 30 seconds on half power. Remove and stir. Repeat at 10-second intervals until the chocolate is just melted. Stir until smooth.

Line a baking sheet with clean parchment paper. Dip an ice cream scoop into the melted chocolate and turn it upside down to remove the excess chocolate. Place the truffles, one at a time, in the scoop and roll around until coated. If using one or more of the toppings, place the truffle into a topping and roll it around to coat, leaving in the topping for 10 to 15 seconds before removing it. Place on the baking sheet. Repeat until all the truffles are coated.

Let the truffles harden in a cool, dry place for at least 1 hour. Store in an airtight container in the refrigerator.

When you are ready to eat, let the miracle berry tablet dissolve on your tongue and then enjoy the dish.

Replacing 1 cup of sugar with 1 tablespoon agave nectar
and the sweetness of the berry saves 47 calories per serving.

Jelly Donut Trifles

MAKES 4 INDIVIDUAL OR 1 LARGE TRIFLE (4 SERVINGS)

In this recipe there are few components that work together to sweeten the dish. The slightly sour notes from the yeast in the donuts works with raspberries, and the balsamic vinegar ties the coffee and jam together.

Ingredients

1 ½ cups cold heavy cream

1 tablespoon instant coffee powder or granules

¾ cup Raspberry Jam (page 256)

¼ cup balsamic vinegar

4 Homemade Donuts (page 29)

1 pint fresh raspberries

Directions

Pour the cream into a large bowl. With an electric mixer, beat on low speed until thick, about 1 minute. Add the coffee and continue to beat until the cream is very thick and soft peaks form. In a separate bowl, combine the Raspberry Jam and balsamic vinegar.

To assemble each trifle, crumble 1 donut into bite-size pieces. Layer one-third of crumbles in the bottom of a parfait or deep glass. Top with a layer of jam, a handful of raspberries, and a layer of whipped cream. Repeat twice more, ending with the cream.

When you are ready to eat, let the miracle berry tablet dissolve on your tongue and then enjoy the dish.

Replacing 1 ½ cups of sugar from the whipped cream and ⅔ cup of sugar from the Raspberry Jam with the sweetness from the berry saves 416 calories per serving.

Peach Puffs

MAKES 8 PUFFS (8 SERVINGS)

These puffs are quite versatile and can be filled with a wide variety of the jams and ice creams in this book instead of the peaches. The filling here is sweetened with lime juice.

Ingredients

Canola oil spray

1 cup water

8 tablespoons (1 stick) unsalted butter

1 cup unbleached all-purpose flour

3 large eggs

1 cup finely diced peeled ripe peaches

3 cups freshly squeezed lime juice

Directions

Preheat the oven to 450 degrees F. Spray a baking sheet with canola oil.

In a large saucepan, bring the water to a boil. Add the butter and stir until melted. Add the flour and stir vigorously until the mixture leaves the sides of the pan and begins to form a stiff ball. Remove from the heat and beat in the eggs one at a time, beating well after each addition. Beat until the batter begins to lose its gloss.

Scoop heaping tablespoons of the batter onto the baking sheet 4 inches apart. Bake for 5 minutes. Making sure not to open the oven door. turn down the oven temperature to 350 degrees F and bake for another 30 minutes, until puffed and deep golden brown. Allow to cool at room temperature.

In a microwave-safe bowl, heat the peaches and lime juice for 3 minutes on medium power.

Using a sharp knife, cut each puff in half horizontally. Fill with peach mixture and serve immediately.

When you are ready to eat, let the miracle berry tablet dissolve on your tongue and then enjoy the dish.

Replacing ¾ cup of sugar with the sweetness from the berry saves 72 calories per serving.

Lemon–Cream Cheese Éclairs

MAKES 20 ÉCLAIRS (10 SERVINGS)

I like to make miniature éclairs—they remind me of the pastries in France. These creamy delicacies are great with coffee and make a fantastic breakfast.

Éclair Shells

8 tablespoons (1 stick) unsalted butter	1 cup unbleached all-purpose flour
1 cup water	¼ teaspoon salt
	4 large eggs

Lemon–Cream Cheese Filling

8 ounces reduced-fat cream cheese	1 tablespoon pure vanilla extract
1 cup cold heavy cream	⅓ cup honey
1 cup freshly squeezed lemon juice	

Directions

Preheat the oven to 450 degrees F. Grease a baking sheet.

TO MAKE THE ÉCLAIR SHELLS: In a medium saucepan, combine the butter and water. Bring to a boil, stirring until butter melts completely. Turn down the heat to low and add flour and salt. Stir vigorously until the mixture leaves the sides of the pan and begins to form a stiff ball. Remove from the heat. Add the eggs one at a time, beating well to incorporate completely after each addition. Beat until the dough begins to lose its gloss.

Transfer the dough to a pastry bag fitted with a No. 10 or larger tip, or to a heavy-duty resealable plastic bag. If using a plastic bag, push the dough to one corner and snip off the corner of the bag. Pipe dough onto cookie sheet in 4 by 1 ½-inch strips.

Bake for 15 minutes. Making sure not to open the oven door, turn down the oven temperature to 325 degrees F and bake for 20 minutes more until golden brown. The éclairs shells should sound hollow when lightly tapped on the bottom.

Transfer the shells to a wire rack to cool completely. When cool, poke a small hole in the short side of each éclair shell.

TO MAKE THE FILLING: With an electric mixer, combine the cream cheese, cream, lemon juice, vanilla, and honey. Whip until stiff peaks form. Fill a pastry bag or a heavy-duty resealable plastic bag with the filling. Twist the bag to get all the filling into the bottom or into one corner. If using a plastic bag, push the dough to one corner and snip off a small corner of the bag. Pipe filling into each éclair. Serve immediately.

When you are ready to eat, let the miracle berry tablet dissolve on your tongue and then enjoy the dish.

Replacing 3 cups of sugar with the sweetness from the berry saves 196 calories per serving.

Pavlova with Berries

MAKES 6 TO 8 SERVINGS

Berries take on such a delicate sweetness—even the tartest ones will taste like they were picked at their peak.

Ingredients

3 large egg whites

Pinch of salt

¼ cup honey

2 tablespoons agave nectar

1 tablespoon cornstarch

1 tablespoon plus ⅓ cup freshly squeezed lemon juice

1 ¼ cups cold heavy cream

2 cups fresh berries such as raspberries, blackberries, or strawberries

Directions

Preheat the oven to 300 degrees F. Line a baking sheet with parchment paper. Draw a 9-inch circle on the parchment with a pencil. (An easy way to do this is to draw around the outside of a 9-inch pan or plate.) Flip the piece of parchment so the drawing is on the bottom and shows through.

With an electric mixer, in a large bowl beat the egg whites and salt on high speed until soft peaks form. Add the honey and agave nectar gradually while continuing to whip until stiff peaks form. In a small bowl, mix the cornstarch and 1 tablespoon of the lemon juice until smooth. Fold into the egg whites. Spread a layer of meringue to fit the circle on the parchment, approximately ¼-inch thick. Spoon swirls of the remaining meringue around the edge to form a shallow bowl shape, or transfer the meringue to a pastry bag fitted with a star or plain tip and pipe a raised border around the edge.

Bake for 1 hour. Turn off the oven but leave meringue inside for 30 minutes more. When cool, the meringue should be hard on the outside and slightly moist on the inside.

In a large bowl, whip the cream to stiff peaks. Fold in the remaining ⅓ cup lemon juice. Spread whipped cream over the pavlova and decorate with fresh berries. Serve immediately.

When you are ready to eat, let the miracle berry tablet dissolve on your tongue and then enjoy the dish.

Replacing 1 cup of sugar with ¼ cup of honey
and the sweetness from the berry saves 49 to 66 calories per serving.

Cannoli

The miracle berry transforms the red wine into a port-like flavor, which combines well with the cream cheese. Together, they produce a well-rounded cannoli mouthfeel and flavor. I recommend using cannoli tubes for perfectly shaped cannoli, but you can improvise using 4-inch-long, 1-inch diameter wooden dowels.

Cannoli Shells

2 cups unbleached all-purpose flour, plus more for rolling the dough

1 teaspoon salt

1 ½ teaspoons ground cinnamon

¼ teaspoon ground nutmeg

2 tablespoons vegetable shortening

1 teaspoon honey

2 large egg whites

¾ cup red wine

1 ½ quarts vegetable oil, for deep-frying

Filling

12 ounces reduced-fat cream cheese, softened

1 ½ cups low-fat ricotta cheese

⅓ cup honey

2 teaspoons pure vanilla extract

¾ cup grated unsweetened chocolate

1 tablespoon grated orange zest

Directions

TO MAKE THE SHELLS: In a large bowl, stir together the flour, salt, cinnamon, and nutmeg. Blend in the shortening, honey, and 1 of the egg whites. Add the red wine 1 tablespoon at a time until the mixture forms a ball. Knead the dough in the bowl enough to bring it together. Cover and let rest for 30 minutes.

Heat oil in deep-fryer or large heavy pot to 375 degrees F. Lightly beat the remaining egg white.

Divide the dough into two parts. On a lightly floured surface, roll the dough to ⅛-inch thick. Cut into 4-inch long ovals. Place a cannoli tube onto the oval lengthwise. Roll up the dough, edges overlapping; seal with a dab of egg white.

Fry the cannoli shells two or three at a time until golden brown. Drain on paper towels and cool completely.

TO MAKE THE FILLING: Combine the cream cheese, ricotta, honey, vanilla, chocolate, and orange zest. Chill for at least 30 minutes before filling the shells.

Drain off any excess liquid from the filling. Fill the cooled shells and smooth off the filling at the ends. Keep refrigerated until serving.

When you are ready to eat, let the miracle berry tablet dissolve on your tongue and then enjoy the dish.

Replacing 2 cups of sugar with 1 teaspoon of honey in the shells and ⅓ cup of honey in the filling, plus the sweetness from the berry saves 98 calories per serving.

Struffoli

Struffoli is a classic Italian dessert made of fried dough balls. We've sweetened these with agave nectar, white wine, and lime juice. Make sure the white wine you use is something acidic like a sauvignon blanc or pinot grigio.

Ingredients

2 cups unbleached all-purpose flour, plus more for dusting

Grated zest of 3 large lemons

Grated zest of 1 large orange

3 tablespoons plus ½ cup agave nectar

½ teaspoon fine sea salt

¼ teaspoon baking powder

4 tablespoons (½ stick) unsalted butter, softened

2 large eggs

1 tablespoon dry white wine

1 teaspoon pure vanilla extract

¼ cup freshly squeezed lemon juice

Canola oil, for deep-frying

Directions

In a food processor, pulse together the flour, lemon and orange zests, 3 tablespoons of the agave nectar, the salt, and baking powder. Add the butter and pulse until the mixture resembles coarse meal. Add the eggs, wine, and vanilla and pulse until the mixture forms into a ball. Wrap the dough in plastic wrap and refrigerate for 30 minutes.

In a large bowl, whisk the remaining ½ cup agave nectar and the lemon juice until combined.

Fill a large saucepan to one-third its depth with canola oil. Heat over medium heat to 375 degrees F. Line a baking sheet with paper towels.

Working in batches, pull the dough into 1-inch balls. Fry the balls of dough until lightly golden, 2 to 3 minutes. Transfer to the paper towels to drain. Toss in agave glaze while still hot and serve.

When you are ready to eat, let the miracle berry tablet dissolve on your tongue and then enjoy the dish.

Replacing 1 ⅔ cup of sugar with ½ cup plus 3 tablespoons of agave nectar and the sweetness from the berry saves 62 to 78 calories per serving.

Yogurt-Covered Soft Pretzels

MAKES 12 PRETZELS (12 SERVINGS)

These are sort of unusual, but lots of fun. The yogurt sauce gives these pretzels plenty of sweetness.

Ingredients

1 ½ cups warm water (110 degrees F)

1 tablespoon honey

2 teaspoons kosher salt

One ¼-ounce package active dry yeast (2 ¼ teaspoons)

4 ½ cups whole-wheat flour

4 tablespoons (½ stick) unsalted butter, melted

Vegetable oil, for the bowl, baking sheets, and work surface

2 ½ quarts plus 1 tablespoon water

⅔ cup baking soda

1 large egg yolk

Pretzel salt or additional kosher salt

Yogurt Sauce (recipe follows)

Directions

Combine the warm water, honey, and kosher salt in the bowl of an electric stand mixer and sprinkle the yeast on top. Allow to sit for 5 minutes or until the mixture begins to foam. Add the flour and butter and using the dough hook, mix on low speed until well combined. Increase the speed to medium and knead the dough until it is smooth and pulls away from the side of the bowl, 4 to 5 minutes.

Remove the dough from the bowl, clean the bowl, and oil it well with vegetable oil. Return the dough to the bowl, cover with plastic wrap, and let sit in a warm place for approximately 1 hour, or until the dough has doubled in size.

Preheat the oven to 450 degrees F. Line two baking sheets with parchment paper and lightly brush with vegetable oil. Bring 2 ½ quarts water and the baking soda to a rolling boil in an 8-quart saucepan or roasting pan. Beat the egg yolk with the remaining 1 tablespoon water to make an egg wash.

Turn out the dough onto a lightly oiled work surface and divide into eight equal pieces. Roll out each piece into a 24-inch-long rope. Make a U shape with a rope. Holding the ends of the rope, cross them over each other and press onto the bottom of the U to form the classic pretzel shape. Place on a baking sheet. Shape the remaining ropes.

Drop the pretzels into the boiling water, one at a time, for 30 seconds. Remove from the water using a large, flat, slotted spatula and return to the baking sheet. Brush the top of each pretzel with the egg wash and sprinkle with pretzel salt. Bake until dark golden brown, 12 to 14 minutes.

Transfer to a wire rack to cool for at least 5 minutes before serving drizzled with the yogurt sauce. Serve immediately or refrigerate covered with plastic wrap.

Yogurt Sauce

MAKES 2 ¾ CUPS

Ingredients

2 cups plain nonfat yogurt   ½ cup freshly squeezed lemon juice
¼ cup honey

Directions

Mix the yogurt, honey, and lemon juice until well combined.

When you are ready to eat, let the miracle berry tablet dissolve on your tongue and then enjoy the dish.

———

Replacing ¾ cup of sugar with 1 tablespoon of honey in the pretzels and ¼ cup of honey in the Yogurt Sauce, plus the sweetness from the berry saves 23 calories per serving.

Sweet Butternut Squash Risotto

MAKES 6 SERVINGS

This is a variation on a dessert we served at Moto. I like to think of it as a dessert rice pudding with butternut squash. The natural sweetness of the squash is amplified by the addition of cream cheese and goat cheese to make a seriously delicious bowl of dessert risotto. If you want to get creative, you can serve this with French toast sticks to give the appearance of garlic bread on the side.

Ingredients

3 cups butternut squash, peeled and cut into ½-inch cubes

1 tablespoon olive oil

1 tablespoon vegetable oil

2 cups Arborio rice

2 cups apple juice (natural, sugar-free)

1 ½ cups water

3 ounces reduced-fat cream cheese

Pinch of salt

3 ounces fresh goat cheese (about ¾ cup)

Directions

Preheat the oven to 400 degrees F.

Toss the squash with the olive oil on a rimmed baking sheet. Roast for 30 minutes, turning once halfway through cooking. Squash should be fork tender when done.

Meanwhile, heat the vegetable oil in a skillet. Stir in the rice and cook for 1 to 2 minutes. Combine apple juice and water and slowly add, ½ cup at a time, stirring frequently and allowing all the liquid to be absorbed before adding more. Continue cooking until the rice is al dente. Stir in the cream cheese and season with a pinch of salt.

After the squash has been cooking for about 25 minutes, crumble the goat cheese into a small baking dish and warm in the oven for 5 minutes, or until the cheese starts to melt and brown along the edges.

Mash half of the squash and stir into the risotto. Ladle the risotto into bowls, and top with the remaining squash cubes and melted goat cheese.

When you are ready to eat, let the miracle berry tablet dissolve on your tongue and then enjoy the dish.

Replacing 2 tablespoons of packed brown sugar and 2 tablespoons of sugar with the sweetness from the berry saves 34 calories per serving.

Paneer with Pineapple and Coconut

One of my favorite creative desserts in this book, this does take some extra work, but the results are so worth it. The sweetness comes from the lemon juice working with the pineapple, which works amazingly well with the paneer (which in turn also lends a nice, subtle sweetness from the buttermilk).

Paneer is a delicate, milky cheese you've probably had in your favorite Indian dishes. It's absolutely delicious in savory stir-fries with spinach or peas, and is a cinch to make at home.

Lime Dipping Sauce

¼ cup freshly squeezed lime juice

¼ cup honey

2 cups Homemade Paneer (recipe follows)

1 cup diced dried pineapple

2 tablespoons freshly squeezed lemon juice

1 large egg yolk

1 cup peanut flour (if you can't find this at your local grocer, try buying online)

Vegetable oil, for frying

1 cup unsweetened shredded coconut

Directions

TO MAKE THE DIPPING SAUCE: In a small bowl, whisk together lime juice and honey.

In a food processor, combine the paneer, pineapple, lemon juice, and egg yolk. Pulse until smooth. Roll into 12 balls and roll in peanut flour.

Heat a pot of frying oil to 275 degrees F. Lightly fry the paneer balls, a few at a time, until golden brown. Drain briefly on paper towels, then roll in coconut. Serve with the dipping sauce.

When you are ready to eat, let the miracle berry tablet dissolve on your tongue and then enjoy the dish.

Homemade Paneer

MAKES 1 BATCH

Ingredients

1 gallon whole milk

1 quart buttermilk

Directions

Line a large colander with several layers of cheesecloth and place the colander in the sink.

In a large saucepan, bring the milk to a boil, being careful not to let it boil over. Stir in the buttermilk. Keep stirring until the liquid separates into curds and whey. Pour into the colander to drain.

When it's cool enough to handle, gather the corners of the cheesecloth into a bundle and squeeze out as much of the excess liquid as you can. Press into a solid cheese and set the bundle in the middle of a plate with a lip (to catch the liquid that will be squeezed out). Put another plate on top and press until the bundle has flattened to a 1-inch-thick disk. Leave the plate on and put something heavy on the plate to weight it down, such as a large can. Let sit at room temperature for 40 to 60 minutes.

Drain off the liquid that has collected and unwrap the paneer. Refrigerate in a closed container until ready to use, as it will firm up even more when chilled.

Replacing ½ cup of sugar with ¼ cup of honey
and the sweetness from the berry saves 32 calories per serving.

Vanilla Ice Cream

MAKES 1 QUART (6 SERVINGS)

The sweetness in this recipe is obtained from the cream cheese, and honey is used to maintain structure.

Ingredients

1 cup heavy cream

2 cups half-and-half

1 vanilla bean, split in half lengthwise

8 large egg yolks

¼ cup honey

⅛ teaspoon salt

8 ounces reduced-fat cream cheese (1 cup)

Directions

Combine the heavy cream and half-and-half in a heavy saucepan. With a small knife, scrape the seeds out of each half of the vanilla bean and add the seeds and pod to the cream mixture. Cook over medium-low heat until barely simmering, stirring frequently. Turn down the heat to low.

Whisk together the egg yolks, honey, and salt in a large bowl until thoroughly combined. Add about ½ cup of the hot cream and whisk vigorously to combine. Repeat three times, whisking thoroughly after each addition. Gradually add the tempered egg yolks back to the hot cream and whisk vigorously to combine. Whisk constantly over medium-low heat until the ice cream base thickens and coats the back of a wooden spoon, 5 to 8 minutes. Do not let the mixture boil.

Using a hand blender, add the cream cheese and blend until smooth. Strain the ice cream base through a fine-mesh strainer into a bowl and refrigerate for about an hour, until cold.

Pour into an ice cream maker and freeze according to the manufacturer's directions.

When you are ready to eat, let the miracle berry tablet dissolve on your tongue and then enjoy the dish.

---

*Replacing 1 cup of sugar with ¼ cup of honey
and the sweetness from the berry saves 86 calories per serving.*

Chocolate Ice Cream

MAKES 1 QUART (6 SERVINGS)

This recipe will certainly have you guessing until you eat it. The texture is really velvety smooth due to the cream cheese and egg yolks. It's perfect with the miracle berry.

Ingredients

1 cup heavy cream

2 cups half-and-half

8 large egg yolks

¼ cup agave nectar

⅛ teaspoon salt

½ cup unsweetened Dutch-process cocoa powder

8 ounces reduced-fat cream cheese (1 cup)

Directions

Combine the heavy cream and half-and-half in a heavy saucepan. Cook over medium-low heat until barely simmering, stirring frequently. Turn down the heat to low.

Whisk together the egg yolks, agave nectar, salt, and cocoa powder in a large bowl until thoroughly combined. Add about ½ cup of the hot cream and whisk vigorously to combine. Repeat three times, whisking thoroughly after each addition. Gradually add the tempered egg yolks back to the hot cream and whisk vigorously to combine. Whisk constantly over medium-low heat until the ice cream base thickens and coats the back of a wooden spoon, 5 to 8 minutes. Do not let the mixture boil.

Using a hand blender, add cream cheese and blend until smooth. Strain the ice cream base through a fine-mesh strainer into a bowl and refrigerate for about an hour, until cold.

Pour into an ice cream maker and freeze according to the manufacturer's directions.

When you are ready to eat, let the miracle berry tablet dissolve on your tongue and then enjoy the dish.

*Replacing 1 ½ cups of sugar with ¼ cup of agave nectar
and the sweetness from the berry saves 152 calories per serving.*

Chocolate Chocolate-Chip Ice Cream

MAKES 1 QUART (6 SERVINGS)

This is a more intense chocolate ice cream than our other recipe. It has added sweetness from the lemon juice.

Ingredients

½ cup freshly squeezed lemon juice

¼ cup unsweetened Dutch-process cocoa powder

1 cup skim milk

2 cups heavy cream

2 large eggs

½ cup agave nectar

2 ounces shaved unsweetened chocolate

Directions

In a small saucepan, bring lemon juice to a boil. Stir in cocoa powder. Turn off the heat.

Combine the milk and cream in a heavy saucepan. Cook over medium-low heat until almost boiling, stirring frequently. Pour a small amount of the cocoa mixture into the milk. Whisk to combine. Gradually pour in the rest of the cocoa mixture. Bring up to almost boiling again.

Beat the eggs in a large bowl. Add about ½ cup of the hot liquid and whisk vigorously to combine. Repeat three times, whisking thoroughly after each addition. Gradually add the tempered eggs back to the hot liquid and whisk vigorously to combine. Stream in the agave nectar and bring back almost to a boil, stirring constantly, until the mixture thickens and coats the back of a wooden spoon, about 5 minutes.

Strain the ice cream base through a fine-mesh strainer into a bowl and refrigerate for about an hour, until cold.

Pour into an ice cream maker and freeze according to the manufacturer's directions.

When the ice cream is almost frozen, fold in the chocolate shavings and place in freezer for at least 2 hours.

When you are ready to eat, let the miracle berry tablet dissolve on your tongue and then enjoy the dish.

Replacing 1 ½ cups of sugar with ½ cup of agave nectar
and the sweetness from the berry saves 112 calories per serving.

Cherry Chocolate Ice Cream

MAKES 1 QUART (6 SERVINGS)

Bing cherries have a natural tartness that works well with the lemon juice to provide sweetness in this recipe.

Ingredients

1 cup skim milk

2 cups heavy cream

2 large eggs

½ cup agave nectar

¼ cup freshly squeezed lemon juice

¼ cup Bing cherries, pitted

¼ cup finely chopped unsweetened chocolate

Directions

Combine the milk and cream in a heavy saucepan. Cook over medium-low heat until almost boiling, stirring frequently.

In a medium bowl, whisk together the eggs and agave nectar. Add about ½ cup of the hot liquid and whisk vigorously to combine. Whisk in a little more of the hot liquid. Gradually add the tempered eggs back into the hot liquid and whisk vigorously to combine. Cook over medium heat, stirring, for about 4 minutes, until the ice cream base thickens and coats the back of a wooden spoon. Stir in the lemon juice.

Strain the ice cream base through a fine-mesh strainer into a bowl and refrigerate for about an hour, until cold.

Pour into an ice cream maker and freeze according to the manufacturer's directions. When the ice cream is almost frozen, fold in the cherries and chocolate.

When you are ready to eat, let the miracle berry tablet dissolve on your tongue and then enjoy the dish.

Replacing 2 cups of sugar with ½ cup of agave nectar
and the sweetness from the berry saves 176 calories per serving.

Strawberry Balsamic Ice Cream

MAKES 1 QUART (6 SERVINGS)

Strawberries and balsamic vinegar are natural friends. In this recipe, we use the acidity from both ingredients—as well as the cream cheese—to naturally sweeten this dessert.

Ingredients

1 cup heavy cream

2 cups half-and-half

¼ cup stemmed and quartered strawberries

8 large egg yolks

¼ cup honey

⅛ teaspoon salt

8 ounces reduced-fat cream cheese (1 cup)

¼ cup balsamic vinegar

Directions

Combine the heavy cream and half-and-half in a heavy saucepan. Add the strawberries and cook over medium-low heat until barely simmering, stirring frequently. Turn down the heat to low.

Whisk together the egg yolks, honey, and salt in a large bowl until thoroughly combined. Slowly pour in about ½ cup of the hot liquid, whisking constantly. Repeat three times, whisking thoroughly before adding each additional ½ cup of hot liquid.

Pour the tempered egg yolks back into the remaining hot liquid, and whisk constantly over medium-low heat until the mixture thickens and coats the back of a wooden spoon, 5 to 8 minutes. Do not let the mixture boil.

Using a hand blender, add cream cheese and blend until smooth. Strain the ice cream base through a fine-mesh strainer into a bowl and stir in the balsamic vinegar. Refrigerate for about an hour, until cold.

Pour into an ice cream maker and freeze according to the manufacturer's directions. Allow to sit in freezer for at least 2 hours.

When you are ready to eat, let the miracle berry tablet dissolve on your tongue and then enjoy the dish.

Replacing 2 cups of sugar with ¼ cup of honey
and the sweetness from the berry saves 214 calories per serving.

Pumpkin Ice Cream

MAKES 1 QUART (6 SERVINGS)

Since pumpkin needs only a small amount of sweetening, we use the acidity from grapefruit juice, which isn't as sweet with the miracle berry as, say, lemon or lime juice.

Ingredients

2 large eggs	1 teaspoon pure vanilla extract
2 large egg yolks	1 ½ teaspoons ground cinnamon
¼ cup agave nectar	1 teaspoon ground ginger
3 cups freshly squeezed grapefruit juice	¼ teaspoon ground nutmeg
	¼ teaspoon salt
⅔ cup canned 100 % pure pumpkin puree	1 ½ cups heavy cream
	½ cup skim milk

Directions

In a large bowl, whisk together the eggs, egg yolks, agave nectar, grapefruit juice, pumpkin, vanilla, cinnamon, ginger, nutmeg, and salt.

Combine the cream and milk in a heavy saucepan. Cook over medium heat until barely simmering, stirring frequently Add one-third of the hot cream to the pumpkin mixture, whisking to combine. Pour the pumpkin mixture back into the cream. Cook over medium heat for about 15 minutes, stirring and scraping the bottom of the pan constantly, until it thickens and coats the back of a wooden spoon. Do not let the mixture boil.

Strain the ice cream base through a fine-mesh sieve into a bowl and refrigerate for about an hour, until cold.

Pour into an ice cream maker and freeze according to the manufacturer's directions.

When you are ready to eat, let the miracle berry tablet dissolve on your tongue and then enjoy the dish.

Replacing 1 cup of sugar with ¼ cup of agave nectar
and the sweetness from the berry saves 188 calories per serving.

Coffee Cake Ice Cream

MAKES 3 QUARTS (18 SERVINGS)

The buttermilk and lime juice are the sweeteners in this recipe. For an extra flavor boost, try adding a teaspoon of ground cardamom—the ice cream will taste like Turkish coffee.

Ingredients

Canola oil spray

2 cups unbleached all-purpose flour, plus more for the pan

1 cup water

3 tablespoons instant coffee powder or granules

½ pound (2 sticks) unsalted butter

¼ cup agave nectar

2 cups freshly squeezed lime juice

¼ teaspoon salt

½ cup low-fat buttermilk

1 large egg

1 teaspoon baking soda

2 teaspoons pure vanilla extract

3 cups half-and-half

2 tablespoons grated lime zest

Directions

Preheat the oven to 350 degrees F. Spray two 9-inch round cake pans with canola oil and sprinkle with flour, tapping out the excess.

Bring the water to a boil in a small saucepan. Add the coffee and stir until dissolved. Melt the butter in another saucepan over medium-low heat. Stir in the dissolved coffee. Add the agave nectar and lime juice and turn off the heat.

In a large bowl, mix the flour and salt. In a separate large bowl, combine the buttermilk, egg, baking soda, and vanilla. Add the butter-coffee mixture and whisk until smooth. Stir in the flour. Divide the batter between the two pans. Bake for 20 to 22 minutes or until set. Cool completely.

In a food processor or blender, working in batches if necessary, puree the cake with the half-and-half and lime zest. Pour into an ice cream maker and freeze according to the manufacturer's directions. Allow to sit in freezer for at least two hours before serving.

When you are ready to eat, let the miracle berry tablet dissolve on your tongue and then enjoy the dish.

Replacing 1 ¼ cups of sugar with ¼ cup of agave nectar
and the sweetness from the berry saves 40 calories per serving.

Tiramisu Ice Cream

MAKES 1 QUART (6 SERVINGS)

Tiramisu gets much of its flavor from sweet Marsala wine. With miracle berries, you don't need to add sweet wine; you can use any dry red wine you like to drink. The lemon juice and cream cheese add the sweetness.

Ingredients

4 large egg yolks

¼ cup agave nectar

¾ cup dry red wine, such as
pinot noir

16 ounces reduced-fat cream cheese,
softened (2 cups)

1 cup cold heavy cream

1 ½ cups brewed espresso

1 tablespoon pure vanilla extract

¼ cup freshly squeezed lemon
juice

Directions

Select a heatproof bowl that will fit over a saucepan like a double boiler. Fill the saucepan with 2 inches of water and bring to a boil. Turn down the heat to a simmer.

Combine the egg yolks and agave nectar in the bowl. Whisk until pale yellow. Place the bowl on top of the saucepan, making sure not to let the bowl touch the water. Gradually whisk in the wine, whisking and scraping the sides of the bowl, and cook for about 5 minutes, until mixture is free of streaks and uniform in color. Remove the bowl from the saucepan, cover with plastic wrap, and refrigerate for 45 minutes.

Whip the cream cheese until smooth. In a separate large bowl, whip the cream until soft peaks form. Gently fold the cream cheese and chilled egg mixture into the whipped cream until incorporated. Cover with plastic wrap and refrigerate for 1 to 2 hours.

Combine the espresso, vanilla, and lemon juice. Stir into ice cream base. Refrigerate again until cold.

Pour into an ice cream maker and freeze according to the manufacturer's directions.

When you are ready to eat, let the miracle berry tablet dissolve on your tongue and then enjoy the dish.

———————————

Replacing 1 cup of sugar with ¼ cup of agave nectar
and the sweetness from the berry saves 88 calories per serving.

Brown Butter–Rosemary Frozen Custard

MAKES 1 QUART (6 SERVINGS)

The combination of nutty browned butter and rosemary is just heavenly in a dessert. Balsamic vinegar adds just the right sweetness.

Ingredients

2 ¼ tablespoons unsalted butter

2 sprigs rosemary

3 cups heavy cream

4 large egg yolks

4 tablespoons balsamic vinegar

Directions

In a saucepan, melt the butter over low heat. Add the rosemary and continue cooking until the butter is brown and nutty in flavor. Remove from the heat and let the rosemary steep for another 2 minutes; discard the rosemary.

Stir in the cream, return to medium heat, and bring to a boil.

In a medium bowl, beat the egg yolks. Add one-third of the hot cream, stirring constantly. Stir the tempered egg yolks back into the hot cream. Cook, stirring, over very low heat until the mixture thickens and coats the back of a wooden spoon. Stir in the vinegar. Strain through a fine-mesh sieve into a bowl and refrigerate for about an hour, until cold.

Pour into an ice cream maker and freeze according to the manufacturer's directions. The custard will still be soft, so transfer to a covered container and freeze for about an hour, until firm enough to scoop. Place in freezer for at least 2 hours before serving.

When you are ready to eat, let the miracle berry tablet dissolve on your tongue and then enjoy the dish.

_____

Replacing 1 cup of sugar with the sweetness from the berry saves 128 calories per serving.

Strawberry Daiquiri Popsicles

Even the sweetest strawberries have a lot of acidity, which pairs nicely with the miracle berries in this fun frozen treat.

Ingredients

4 ½ cups strawberries, stemmed

1 cup plus 2 tablespoons freshly squeezed orange juice

½ cup white rum

Directions

Combine all the ingredients in a blender or food processor. Strain through a fine-mesh strainer to remove the strawberry seeds. Pour into six 4-ounce paper cups and cover tightly with foil. Carefully push popsicle sticks through the foil and freeze for at least 4 hours.

When ready to serve, run slightly warm water over the outside of each cup and peel off the cups to remove the pops.

When you are ready to eat, let the miracle berry tablet dissolve on your tongue and then enjoy the dish.

Replacing ½ cup of sugar with the sweetness from the berry saves 64 calories per serving.

Margarita Popsicles

The refreshing lemon, lime, and orange juices, plus the slight bite of the tequila, make these sugar-free pops sweet and citrusy.

Ingredients

¾ cup freshly squeezed lime juice

½ cup water

¼ cup freshly squeezed lemon juice

2 tablespoons freshly squeezed orange juice

2 tablespoons tequila

1 tablespoon kosher salt (optional)

Directions

Mix together the lime juice, water, lemon and orange juices, and the tequila. Pour into six 4-ounce paper cups and cover tightly with foil. Carefully push popsicle sticks through the foil and freeze for at least 4 hours.

When ready to serve, run slightly warm water over the outside of each cup and peel off the cups to remove the pops. Garnish with the kosher salt, if desired.

When you are ready to eat, let the miracle berry tablet dissolve on your tongue and then enjoy the dish.

Replacing 1 cup of sugar with the sweetness from the berry saves 128 calories per serving.

Watermelon Sorbet

You will find that this recipe has an intense flavor, like the most perfect watermelon you have ever had. Here, the lime juice adds great flavor in addition to sweetness.

Ingredients

8 cups seedless watermelon chunks

Grated zest and juice of 5 limes, plus juice of 2 more limes

2 tablespoons agave nectar

Directions

Place half the watermelon, half the lime juice, half the lime zest, and half the agave nectar in a blender. Process until smooth, then pour into a large bowl. Repeat with other half of ingredients. Combine the two batches. Pour into an ice cream maker and freeze according to the manufacturer's directions. Freeze for two hours before serving.

When you are ready to eat, let the miracle berry tablet dissolve on your tongue and then enjoy the dish.

Replacing 1 ¼ cups of sugar with 2 tablespoons of agave nectar and the sweetness from the berry saves 105 calories per serving.

Coffee Granita

This is a simple treat on a hot summer day. The effect of the miracle berry on coffee is really amazing. It subdues the bitterness and enables more coffee flavor to come through. Along with the sweetness that the lime juice provides, this simple treat is a lot of fun.

Ingredients

2 cups lukewarm espresso or strong black coffee

1 tablespoon agave nectar

¼ cup freshly squeezed lime juice

2 tablespoons coffee liqueur

2 recipes Whipped Cream (page 250), for serving

Directions

Combine the espresso, agave nectar, lime juice, and liqueur in a 13 by 9-inch metal baking pan and stir well. The mixture should only come about ¼ inch up the side of the pan. Place on a level shelf in the freezer for 30 minutes.

Remove from the freezer and use a dinner fork to scrape any ice crystals that have formed on the side or bottom of the pan. Return to freezer. Repeat scraping every 20 to 30 minutes for 3 to 4 hours.

Once mixture is thoroughly frozen, fluff with a fork and allow the ice flakes to sit in the freezer for another 30 minutes before serving.

Scoop into martini glasses and top with unsweetened whipped cream.

When you are ready to eat, let the miracle berry tablet dissolve on your tongue and then enjoy the dish.

---

*Replacing ½ cup of sugar with 1 tablespoon of agave nectar
and the sweetness from the berry saves 54 calories per serving.*

JAMS, SAUCES, AND FROSTINGS

Whipped Cream

Ingredients

⅓ cup cold heavy cream   1 teaspoon honey
Juice from 1½ limes

Directions

In a large bowl, whip the cream until thickened. Add the honey and lime juice. Beat until stiff peaks form.

Removing ½ cup of sugar with 1 teaspoon of honey
and the sweetness from the berry saves 60 calories per serving.

Old-Fashioned Hot Fudge

I guess we can't say this is really old-fashioned, since it uses the miracle berry and lemon juice as the sweetener, but it definitely tastes like classic old-fashioned hot fudge. Perfect on a scoop of ice cream.

Ingredients

¼ cup unbleached all-purpose flour

⅔ cup unsweetened
   Dutch-process cocoa powder

1 ½ cups skim milk

4 tablespoons (½ stick) unsalted
   butter

1 cup honey

1 cup agave nectar

2 teaspoons pure vanilla extract

½ cup freshly squeezed lemon juice

Directions

In a medium bowl, whisk together the flour and cocoa powder. Combine milk, butter, honey, agave nectar, and vanilla in a medium saucepan over medium heat and cook until the butter has melted. Slowly add flour-cocoa mixture, constantly whisking. Bring to a boil, stirring constantly, and cook until thick and smooth, about 5 minutes. Stir in the lemon juice. Cool to lukewarm and serve, or transfer to a container with a cover, let cool, and refrigerate. Refrigerate any unused portion.

NOTE: This can be reheated in a double boiler, or microwaved in 30 second intervals, as needed.

When you are ready to eat, let the miracle berry tablet dissolve on your tongue and then enjoy the dish.

Replacing 3 ½ cups of sugar with 1 cup of honey, 1 cup of agave nectar, and the sweetness from the berry saves 34 calories per serving.

Lemon Curd

Perfect lemon curd has to have the right balance of sweetness and pucker. This creamy, golden filling is delicious with scones or crepes, or atop fresh berries.

Ingredients

2 teaspoons grated lemon zest

¾ cup freshly squeezed lemon juice

¼ cup agave nectar

3 large egg yolks

Pinch of salt

4 tablespoons (½ stick) unsalted
    butter, cut into tablespoons

¼ teaspoon lemon extract

Directions

In a saucepan, whisk together the lemon zest and juice, agave nectar, egg yolks, and salt. Add the butter and cook over medium-low heat, whisking constantly, for about 5 minutes, until the mixture is thick enough to hold the marks of the whisk and first bubbles appear on surface. Whisk in the lemon extract. Pour into a bowl and cover the with plastic wrap or wax paper directly on the surface. Refrigerate until cold, about 30 minutes.

Lemon curd can be stored for up to 3 days in the refrigerator.

When you are ready to eat, let the miracle berry tablet dissolve on your tongue and then enjoy the dish.

*Replacing ¾ cup of sugar with ¼ cup of agave nectar
and the sweetness from the berry saves 68 calories per serving.*

Fresh Cherry Preserves

Cherry preserves are perfect on a bagel or toast. The tartness of the cherries and the lime juice add the perfect amount of sweetness.

Ingredients

6 cups pitted cherries

2 cups freshly squeezed lime juice

1 cup agave nectar

2 tablespoons agave nectar

½ cup powedered pectin

½ teaspoon unsalted butter

Directions

Sterilize three 1-pint jars with lids. Drain but keep warm.

Place the cherries in a Dutch oven. In a separate bowl, mix lime juice and 2 table-spoons of agave nectar. Stir in the pectin and add mixture to the cherries. Add the butter and bring to a boil, stirring. Stir for 1 minute. Remove from the heat and skim off any foam. Add 1 cup of agave nectar and return to a boil. Remove from heat.

Immediately spoon the preserves into the jars. Secure the lids, invert, and let stand for 5 minutes. Turn upright and cool. Refrigerate and store covered with plastic wrap.

When you are ready to eat, let the miracle berry tablet dissolve on your tongue and then enjoy the dish.

Replacing 3 ¼ cups of sugar with 1 cup plus 2 tablespoons of agave nectar and the sweetness from the berry saves 59 calories per serving.

Grape Jelly

MAKES 3 CUPS (24 SERVINGS, 1 TABLESPOON PER SERVING)

Grape jelly is typically loaded with sugar, yet this recipe relies on lemon juice for sweetness. Partnered with unsweetened peanut butter, it's a much-better-for-you PB&J.

Ingredients

2 cups Concord grapes

2 tablespoons raisins

1 cup freshly squeezed lime juice

¼ cup agave nectar

⅓ cup plus ¾ teaspoon powdered
    pectin

Directions

Sterilize three half-pint jars with lids. Drain but keep warm. Thoroughly wash each part of the blender with very hot water and drain upside down.

In a saucepan, combine the grapes, raisins, lime juice, agave nectar, and pectin. While constantly stirring, bring to a slow boil, then turn down the heat and simmer for 10 minutes or until the liquid has reduced by three-quarters, stirring occassionally. Remove from heat and carefully transfer to the blender. Puree for 2 minutes, scraping down the blender twice. Transfer to the jars, seal tightly, and refrigerate.

When you are ready to eat, let the miracle berry tablet dissolve on your tongue and then enjoy the dish.

Replacing 1 ¾ cups of sugar with ¼ cup of agave nectar
and the sweetness from the berry saves 46 calories per serving.

Mango Jam

Mango and lime is a dynamite combination. This jam takes pancakes or waffles to a new level.

Ingredients

3 cups chopped mango

1 cup freshly squeezed lime juice

⅓ cup powdered pectin

1 tablespoon ground cinnamon

1 teaspoon grated lime zest

Directions

Sterilize two half-pint jars with lids. Drain but keep warm. Thoroughly wash each part of the blender with very hot water and drain upside down.

In a medium saucepan, bring the mango, lime juice, and pectin to a boil. While constantly stirring, turn down the heat to a simmer and cook for 20 minutes. Carefully transfer mixture to a blender and puree for 2 minutes, making sure to scrape down the sides of the blender twice. Stir in the cinnamon and lime zest. Pour into the jars, secure the lids, and let cool.

When you are ready to eat, let the miracle berry tablet dissolve on your tongue and then enjoy the dish.

Replacing ½ cup of sugar with the sweetness from the berry saves 24 calories per serving.

Raspberry Jam

It doesn't get much simpler than this recipe. Raspberry and lemon juice, that's it. You'll never buy jam again.

Ingredients

1 cup raspberries

1 cup freshly squeezed lemon juice

Directions

Sterilize two half-pint jars with lids. Drain but keep warm. Thoroughly wash each part of the blender with very hot water and drain upside down.

In a small saucepan over medium heat, combine the raspberries and lemon juice. Cook until only one-quarter of the liquid remains. Pour into a blender or food processor and puree until smooth. Strain to remove the raspberry seeds, if desired. Pour into jars, secure the lids, and let cool.

When you are ready to eat, let the miracle berry tablet dissolve on your tongue and then enjoy the dish.

Replacing ⅔ cup of sugar with the sweetness from the berry saves 64 calories per serving.

Spiced Cherry Jam

This is a totally fun recipe. Pickle juice is tangy, sour, a little spicy, and absolutely delicious with cherries.

Ingredients

3 cups dried cherries, chopped

2 cups Sweet Pickle Juice (page 261)

1 tablespoon grated lemon zest

Directions

Sterilize two half-pint jars with lids. Drain but keep warm. Thoroughly wash each part of the blender with very hot water and drain upside down.

Soak the cherries in the pickle juice for 1 to 2 hours.

Transfer to a saucepan and bring to a boil. Simmer until the juice has reduced by half. Remove from heat. Stir in lemon zest.

Drain the cherries, reserving the juice. Puree the cherries in a blender or food processor, adding reserved liquid as needed. Pour into jars, secure the lids, and let cool.

When you are ready to eat, let the miracle berry tablet dissolve on your tongue and then enjoy the dish.

Replacing 2 cups of sugar with the sweetness from the berry saves 48 calories per serving.

Almond Paste

Lime juice provides the sweetness in this recipe.

Ingredients

1 ½ cups raw blanched almonds

⅔ cup agave nectar

¼ cup water

¼ cup freshly squeezed lime juice, plus more if needed

2 tablespoons honey

4 tablespoons (½ stick) unsalted butter, melted

Directions

In a food processor, grind the almonds until coarsely chopped. In a saucepan, combine the agave nectar, water, lime juice, and honey. Bring to a boil. Remove from heat and carefully pour into the ground almonds. Streaming in the melted butter, puree until smooth. This may take 10 minutes or more, depending on the strength of the food processor. If the mixture is too thick, slowly add more lime juice until desired consistency is reached. Store in refrigerator covered with plastic.

When you are ready to eat, let the miracle berry tablet dissolve on your tongue and then enjoy the dish.

Replacing 1 ¾ cups of sugar with ⅔ cup of agave nectar, 2 tablespoons of honey, and the sweetness from the berry saves 72 calories per serving.

Banana-Walnut Spread

MAKES 1 ½ CUPS (10 SERVINGS, A LITTLE LESS THAN 2 ½ TABLESPOONS PER
SERVING)

Lemon juice sweetens this paste, which is perfect for filling crepes or spreading on toast.

Ingredients

2 bananas, sliced

Grated zest and juice of 1 lemon

1 cup walnut pieces

Directions

In a small nonstick saucepan, cook the bananas until soft. Stir in the lemon zest and juice and remove from the heat. In a food processor, coarsely chop the walnuts. Add the banana mixture and puree until smooth. Refrigerate covered with plastic wrap.

When you are ready to eat, let the miracle berry tablet dissolve on your tongue and then enjoy the dish.

Replacing ½ cup of sugar with the sweetness from the berry saves 39 calories per serving.

Raisin Nut Spread

MAKES 3 ½ CUPS (35 SERVINGS, A LITTLE MORE THAN 1 ½ TABLESPOONS PER SERVING)

This spread gets its sweetness from lemon juice. It is a great spread on toast or a flour tortilla. Try it and you'll agree.

Ingredients

1 ½ cups unsalted raw cashews

1 ½ cups blanched almonds

1 ½ teaspoons ground cinnamon

½ teaspoon salt

2 tablespoons raisins

6 tablespoons freshly squeezed lemon juice

About 2 tablespoons freshly squeezed orange juice

Directions

Preheat the oven to 375 degrees F. Spread the cashews and almonds on a baking sheet in a single layer. Toast for 10 minutes, stirring halfway through the cooking. Remove from the oven and let cool.

In a blender or food processor, puree the nuts, cinnamon, salt, raisins, and lemon juice. Gradually add orange juice until the desired consistency is reached. Refrigerate covered with plastic wrap.

When you are ready to eat, let the miracle berry tablet dissolve on your tongue and then enjoy the dish.

Replacing 1 cup of packed brown sugar with the sweetness from the berry saves 24 calories per serving.

Sweet Pickle Juice

In this recipe, we use white wine vinegar for the acidity, which provides sweetness with the miracle berry.

Ingredients

1 ½ quarts water

2 cups white wine vinegar

3 cups agave nectar

2 tablespoons coriander seeds

1 tablespoons crushed red pepper flakes

2 tablespoons mustard seeds

1 tablespoon cumin seeds

1 tablespoon fennel seeds

3 tablespoons pink peppercorns

Directions

Combine all ingredients in a large saucepan. Bring to a boil, turn down the heat and simmer for 20 minutes. Strain and allow to cool.

Refrigerate in covered container.

When you are ready to eat, let the miracle berry tablet dissolve on your tongue and then enjoy the dish.

Replacing 4 cups of sugar with 3 cups of agave nectar and the sweetness of the berry saves 192 total calories (or 24 calories per cup).

Chocolate Sour Cream Frosting

MAKES 5 CUPS

This frosting obtains sweetness from both the lime juice and sour cream.

Ingredients

12 ounces unsweetened chocolate, chopped

¾ pound (3 sticks) unsalted butter, softened

¾ cup agave nectar

1 cup freshly squeezed lime juice

1 cup low-fat sour cream

Pinch of kosher salt

Directions

Melt the chocolate in the top of a double boiler or a heatproof bowl set over (not in) simmering water, stirring often, until smooth. Remove from the heat and let cool for 10 to 15 minutes.

With an electric mixer, beat the butter on high speed until light and fluffy, 3 to 5 minutes. Turn down the mixer speed to low. Gradually add the agave nectar and lime juice and beat until smooth, scraping down the sides of the bowl as necessary. Add the chocolate, sour cream, and salt and beat until thoroughly combined and smooth. Refrigerate covered in plastic wrap.

When you are ready to eat, let the miracle berry tablet dissolve on your tongue and then enjoy the dish.

_Replacing 2 ½ cups of sugar with ¾ cup of agave nectar
and the sweetness from the berry saves 240 calories per cup._

Chocolate Buttercream Frosting

This buttercream get its sweetness from the addition of lime juice.

Ingredients

4 ounces finely chopped unsweetened chocolate

¼ cup hot strong brewed coffee

8 tablespoons (1 stick) unsalted butter, softened

2 tablespoons agave nectar

4 large egg yolks (pasteurized)

¼ cup freshly squeezed lime juice

Directions

In a small bowl combine the chocolate and coffee. Let sit for 1 to 2 minutes. Whisk until smooth.

With an electric mixer, beat the butter and agave nectar until creamy. Add the egg yolks, lime juice and melted chocolate and beat until smooth and creamy. Refrigerate covered with plastic wrap.

When you are ready to eat, let the miracle berry tablet dissolve on your tongue and then enjoy the dish.

---

*Replacing ¾ cup of sugar with 2 tablespoons of agave nectar
and the sweetness from the berry saves 228 calories per cup.*

Mocha Frosting

The sweetness in this recipe comes from the lime juice and sour cream. The sour cream provides a nice texture, as well.

Ingredients

1 cup heavy cream

1 teaspoon finely ground espresso coffee

1 cup unsweetened Dutch-process cocoa powder

10 ounces chopped unsweetened chocolate

1 tablespoon coffee liqueur (optional)

1 teaspoon pure vanilla extract

½ cup freshly squeezed lime juice

1 cup low-fat or nonfat sour cream

Directions

In a large saucepan, heat the heavy cream and espresso grounds over medium heat, stirring occasionally, until the mixture bubbles around the edges, 2 to 3 minutes. Remove from heat, add the cocoa powder and chocolate and stir until the chocolate is melted and the mixture is smooth. Stir in the liqueur, if using, the vanilla, and lime juice. Transfer to a large bowl, cover loosely, and refrigerate for 2 hours.

If mixture has become too hard to beat, heat in a microwave oven in 10-second intervals until soft but not melted. Add the sour cream and beat with an electric mixer on high speed until combined. Refrigerate covered with plastic wrap.

When you are ready to eat, let the miracle berry tablet dissolve on your tongue and then enjoy the dish.

Replacing 2 ½ cups of sugar with the sweetness from the berry saves 480 calories per cup.

Vanilla Frosting

This recipe has a subtle sweetness obtained from the grapefruit juice.

Ingredients

5 tablespoons unbleached
all-purpose flour

1 cup skim milk

1 teaspoon pure vanilla extract

¾ cup freshly squeezed grapefruit
juice

½ pound (2 sticks) unsalted butter,
melted

¼ cup agave nectar

¼ cup grated lime zest

Directions

In a small saucepan, beat the flour into the milk over medium heat, whisking constantly, until the milk thickens. Remove from the heat and let cool to room temperature.

Stir in the vanilla and grapefruit juice. With an electric mixer, combine the butter and agave nectar. Add the milk-flour-juice mixture and beat until well-combined and fluffy, resembling whipped cream. Fold in the lime zest.

Refrigerate covered in plastic wrap.

When you are ready to eat, let the miracle berry tablet dissolve on your tongue and then enjoy the dish.

Replacing 1 ½ cups of sugar with ¼ cup of agave nectar
and the sweetness of the berry saves 456 calories per cup.

Lemon Buttercream Frosting

This recipe obtains sweetness and flavor from the lemon juice.

Ingredients

½ pound (2 sticks) unsalted butter, softened

¾ cup agave nectar

½ cup freshly squeezed lemon juice

½ teaspoon lemon extract

2 teaspoons grated lemon zest

Directions

With an electric mixer, beat the butter on high speed until light and fluffy, about 1 minute. Turn down the mixer speed to low and add agave nectar, lemon juice, lemon extract, and lemon zest. Mix until creamy and smooth, about 2 minutes. Refrigerate covered with plastic wrap.

When you are ready to eat, let the miracle berry tablet dissolve on your tongue and then enjoy the dish.

Replacing 1 ¾ cups of sugar with ¾ cup of agave nectar
and the sweetness from the berry saves 312 calories per cup.

Cream Cheese Frosting

MAKES 3 CUPS

The cream cheese provides sweetness and texture while the lime juice provides additional sweetness.

Ingredients

1 teaspoon unflavored powdered gelatin

¼ cup freshly squeezed lime juice

2 ¾ cups reduced-fat cream cheese

2 tablespoons agave nectar

Directions

Sprinkle the gelatin over the lime juice and let sit for 5 to 10 minutes to bloom.

In a saucepan, whisk together the cream cheese, agave nectar, and bloomed gelatin. Heat until smooth. Remove from the heat. Let cool slightly.

When you are ready to eat, let the miracle berry tablet dissolve on your tongue and then enjoy the dish.

---

*Replacing 2 ¾ cups of sugar with 2 tablespoons of agave nectar
and the sweetness from the berry saves 664 calories per cup.*

Mascarpone Frosting

This is a simple recipe that uses lime juice as the sweetener.

Ingredients

1 ½ cups cold heavy cream

3 tablespoons agave nectar

1 cup mascarpone cheese, softened

3 tablespoons grated lime zest

¼ cup freshly squeezed lime juice

Directions

With an electric mixer, in a large bowl whip the cream with the agave nectar until soft peaks form. Gently fold in the mascarpone, lime zest, and lime juice.

When you are ready to eat, let the miracle berry tablet dissolve on your tongue and then enjoy the dish.

Replacing 1 cup of sugar with 3 tablespoons of agave nectar and the sweetness from the berry saves 168 calories per cup.

Goat Cheese Frosting

MAKES 3 CUPS

This frosting recipe uses goat cheese and lemon juice for sweetening.

Ingredients

1 ½ cups fresh goat cheese (6 ounces), softened

1 cup skim milk

¼ teaspoon salt

½ cup freshly squeezed lemon juice

Directions

With an electric mixer, beat the goat cheese, milk, salt, and lemon juice until creamy.

When you are ready to eat, let the miracle berry tablet dissolve on your tongue and then enjoy the dish.

Replacing ⅔ cup of sugar with the sweetness from the berry saves 171 calories per cup.

Raspberry Icing

The raspberries have a natural tartness that creates a slightly sweetened profile and the lime juice increases that sweetness.

Ingredients

1 teaspoon unflavored powdered gelatin

1 cup freshly squeezed lime juice

1 cup half-and-half

3 cups fresh raspberries

¼ cup agave nectar

Directions

Sprinkle the gelatin over the lime juice and let sit for 5 to 10 minutes to bloom.

In a saucepan, bring the half-and-half and raspberries to a boil. Lower the heat and simmer for 4 minutes. Stir in the lime juice and gelatin. Transfer to a blender and puree until smooth. Strain to remove raspberry seeds. Stir in the agave nectar until smooth.

Refrigerate and cover with plastic wrap.

When you are ready to eat, let the miracle berry tablet dissolve on your tongue and then enjoy the dish.

---

*Replacing 1 ¾ cups of sugar with ¼ cup of agave nectar
and the sweetness from the berry saves 552 calories per cup.*

FLAVOR-TRIPPING

COCKTAILS

ocktails are one of my favorite treats on miracle berries. At iNG, we have become well known not only for flavor-tripping meals, but cocktails that start out tasting like one drink then transform into another, different cocktail. Pretty mind-blowing.

One example is a classic gin and tonic. We remove the tonic water and use soda water and lime. Before eating the miracle berry, it tastes like a standard gin and tonic, but after, it morphs into a Sloe Gin Screw. Here we accentuate the orange-like flavors limes can deliver with the right usage.

There are tons of amazing flavor-changing combinations to explore. While I'd prefer you to come to iNG and let us demonstrate them for you, here are a number of flavor-tripping concoctions you can whip up on your own.

Beer and wine, too, can be fascinating gateways into miracle berry creativity. Some beers will taste wildly sweet. Stouts can taste like chocolate milk (maybe a splash on an adult float?) Ales can taste less nutty and more fruity, and dry, hoppy lagers will taste more complex and very robust.

Wines take on their own new lives as well. If you are a fan of riesling, Madeira, sweet sherry, port, or any slightly sweet wine, you are in luck. Dry white wine will taste like fruity riesling or off-dry grüner veltliner. Red wine will taste more like port, sweet sherry, or Madeira. Lots of fun, and very economical.

No matter how you decide to approach the beverage component, you will have a ton of fun clearing out your liquor cabinet while you discover these new worlds in flavor.

"Gin and Tonic" to Sloe Gin Screw

MAKES 1 COCKTAIL

This is a cocktail that we have served at iNG, a sugarless gin and tonic. Drink half of this prior to eating the miracle berry. After eating the berry, the lime juice starts to taste like orange, thus changing into a sloe gin screw. Tons of fun.

Ingredients

Ice cubes

1 jigger (1 ½ ounces) sloe gin

3 ounces club soda
 (do not use tonic water)

½ jigger (¾ ounce) freshly squeezed
 lime juice

Wedge of lime

Directions

Fill a highball glass halfway with ice. Add the gin, club soda, and lime juice. Stir, and garnish with lime.

When you are ready to drink, let the miracle berry tablet dissolve on your tongue and then enjoy the beverage.

Replacing 1 tablespoon of sugar with the sweetness from the berry saves 48 calories per cocktail.

Champagne Fizz to "Lemon Drop"

MAKES 1 COCKTAIL

This is my version of a French 75. The combination of Champagne, gin, and fresh lemon juice is refreshing and light and very festive. The sweetness comes from both the Champagne and lemon juice. So enjoy half of this cocktail before (Champagne Fizz) and the rest after you eat the miracle berry (Lemon Drop).

Ingredients

Ice cubes	1 ounce freshly squeezed lemon juice
1 ½ ounces gin	3 ounces chilled Champagne

Directions

Fill a cocktail shaker halfway with ice. Add the gin and lemon juice and shake until chilled. Strain into a champagne flute and top with Champagne.

When you are ready to drink, let the miracle berry tablet dissolve on your tongue and then enjoy the beverage.

Replacing 2 teaspoons of sugar with the sweetness from the berry saves 32 calories per cocktail.

Skinny Margarita

MAKES 2 COCKTAILS

There is nothing more festive and refreshing than a classic margarita. Everyone loves them, but they are loaded with sugar. The different juices in this recipe add layers of flavor but none of the sugar. For an even lighter version of a margarita, top with 2 ounces of club soda.

Ingredients

Wedge of lime (optional)

Coarse salt (optional)

Ice cubes

2 ounces tequila

2 ounces freshly squeezed lime juice

2 ounces freshly squeezed lemon juice

2 ounces freshly squeezed orange juice

Directions

If you like your margaritas with salt, prep two margarita glasses by rubbing the rims with a wedge of lime and dipping into coarse salt.

Fill a cocktail shaker halfway with ice. Add the tequila and lime, lemon, and orange juices. Cover tightly and, using a towel over the top, shake vigorously until the outside of the shaker is covered with frost. Strain into the glasses.

When you are ready to drink, let the miracle berry tablet dissolve on your tongue and then enjoy the beverage.

Replacing ⅓ cup of sugar with the sweetness from the berry saves 129 calories per cocktail.

Lemon Drop

MAKES 1 COCKTAIL

A very simple recipe here. This can be served as a refreshing aperitif or after-dinner cocktail with the Lemon Poppy Seed Cake on page 110. Either way, it's a winner.

Ingredients

Ice cubes

½ jigger (¾ ounce)
   freshly squeezed lemon juice

1 jigger (1 ½ ounces) vodka

Twist of lemon zest

Directions

Chill a cocktail glass in the freezer at least 20 minutes before serving. Fill a cocktail shaker halfway with ice. Add the lemon juice and vodka. Cover tightly and shake vigorously until the outside of the shaker is covered with frost. Strain into the chilled glass and garnish with the lemon zest.

When you are ready to drink, let the miracle berry tablet dissolve on your tongue and then enjoy the beverage.

Replacing 2 teaspoons of sugar with the sweetness from the berry saves 32 calories per cocktail.

Chocolate Martini

For a truly special chocolate martini, you have to make your own Cocoa Vodka. The complex cocoa flavor simply can't be achieved with a premade product. Make a big batch and use it for weeks, it will only get better as it has more time to infuse.

Ingredients

Ice cubes

1 jigger (1 ½ ounces) Cocoa Vodka (recipe follows)

½ jigger (¾ ounce) freshly squeezed orange juice

½ jigger (¾ ounce) freshly squeezed lemon juice

Ice

Directions

Fill a cocktail shaker halfway with ice. Add the vodka, orange juice, and lemon juice. Cover tightly and shake vigorously until the outside of the shaker is covered with frost. Strain into a cocktail glass.

Cocoa Vodka

MAKES ENOUGH FOR ABOUT 16 COCKTAILS

Ingredients

2 cups cocoa nibs

One 750-milliliter bottle vodka

Directions

Combine cocoa nibs and vodka in an airtight container. Shake bottle once a day and allow to sit at room temperature for 1 week before using.

When ready to use, pour desired amount through a strainer and return the nibs to the rest of the vodka.

When you are ready to drink, let the miracle berry tablet dissolve on your tongue and then enjoy the beverage.

Replacing ¼ cup of sugar with the sweetness from the berry saves 192 calories per cocktail.

Dirty Martini

MAKES 1 COCKTAIL

Every time we serve this at the restaurant, our customers tell us it's the best martini they have ever had. Try it for yourself—it's clean and complex.

Ingredients

Ice cubes

2 ounces vodka

1 ounce green olive juice

Directions

Chill a martini glass in the freezer for at least 20 minutes before serving.

Fill a cocktail shaker halfway with ice. Add vodka and olive juice. Shake or stir for 10 seconds. Strain into the chilled glass.

When you are ready to drink, let the miracle berry tablet dissolve on your tongue and then enjoy the beverage.

Replacing the dry vermouth with the sweetness from the berry saves 20 calories per cocktail.

Strawberry Frozen Daiquiri

A well-made strawberry daiquiri should not be overly sweet, but allow you to taste all of the flavors of the lime juice and rum. To whip up a batch of virgin daiquiris, simply eliminate the rum.

Ingredients

2 ounces light rum

5 fresh strawberries, stemmed

½ ounce freshly squeezed lemon

½ ounce freshly squeezed lime juice

½ ounce freshly squeezed orange juice

1 cup crushed ice

Directions

Chill a 12-ounce glass in the freezer for at least an hour before serving. Place all ingredients in a blender and puree until smooth. Serve in the chilled glass.

When you are ready to drink, let the miracle berry tablet dissolve on your tongue and then enjoy the beverage.

Replacing the strawberry schnapps and superfine sugar with the sweetness from the berry saves 60 calories per cocktail, and replacing 2 tablespoons of sugar with the sweetness from the berry saves 96 calories per cocktail, for a total of 156 calories per cocktail.

Piña Colada

The already intense flavors in a piña colada are mind-blowing with miracle berries. Tropical fruits, which are grown where miracle berries grow, make perfect partners.

Ingredients

1 cup crushed ice

2 ounces coconut-flavored rum, such as Malibu

2 ounces pineapple juice

1 ounce freshly squeezed orange juice

1 ounce freshly squeezed lemon juice

1 ½ ounces unsweetened coconut milk

Wedge of fresh pineapple

1 fresh cherry

Directions

Chill a highball glass in the freezer for at least an hour before serving. Combine the ice, rum, pineapple, orange, and lemon juices, and coconut milk in a blender and puree until smooth. Serve in the chilled glass, garnished with the pineapple and cherry.

When you are ready to drink, let the miracle berry tablet dissolve on your tongue and then enjoy the beverage.

Replacing 2 teaspoons of sugar with the sweetness from the berry saves 32 calories per cocktail.

Mojito

The key to a great mojito is really muddling the mint. Since there is no granulated sugar to break down the mint leaves, use the lime wedges and a muddler or the end of a wooden spoon to really crush the leaves and release their essential oils.

Ingredients

15 small or 7 large mint leaves

Half a lime, cut into wedges

Ice cubes

2 ounces white rum

½ ounce freshly squeezed lemon juice

3 ounces club soda

Directions

Place the mint leaves and lime wedges in the bottom of a highball glass. Muddle the mint and lime together. Fill the glass halfway with ice. Pour in the rum and lemon juice and top with the club soda.

When you are ready to drink, let the miracle berry tablet dissolve on your tongue and then enjoy the beverage.

Replacing 2 tablespoons of sugar with the sweetness from the berry saves 96 calories per cocktail.

Greyhound

MAKES 1 COCKTAIL

Classic cocktails have definitely made a comeback. If you have never tried a Greyhound, it's time to revisit this retro favorite. The old-school Greyhound is made with gin and grapefruit juice, but it's very bitter. Lots of modern versions add simple syrup to make it a little more palatable. The lemon juice in this one with the miracle berries has perfect balance.

Ingredients

Ice cubes

2 ounces vodka

4 ounces freshly squeezed grapefruit juice

1 ounce freshly squeezed lemon juice

Directions

Fill a highball glass halfway with ice. Add the vodka, grapefruit juice, and lemon juice. Stir.

When you are ready to drink, let the miracle berry tablet dissolve on your tongue and then enjoy the beverage.

Replacing 1 tablespoon of sugar with the sweetness from the berry saves 48 calories per cocktail.

7 & 7

MAKES 1 COCKTAIL

The 7 & 7 has never been my favorite drink . . . well, that is, not until I turned it into a flavor-tripping drink.

Ingredients

Ice cubes

2 ounces Seagram's 7 blended
   whiskey

1 ounce freshly squeezed lemon juice

1 ounce freshly squeezed lime juice

3 ounces club soda

Lemon wedge

Directions

Fill a highball glass halfway with ice. Add the whiskey and lemon and lime juices, and top with club soda. Garnish with a wedge of lemon.

When you are ready to drink, let the miracle berry tablet dissolve on your tongue and then enjoy the beverage.

Replacing 2 tablespoons of sugar with the sweetness from the berry saves 96 calories per cocktail.

Creamsicle

MAKES 1 COCKTAIL

This drink is good on the rocks, but it's also delicious blended. Either way, make sure to serve in a frozen glass.

Ingredients

Ice cubes

2 ounces vanilla vodka

2 ounces freshly squeezed
orange juice

2 ounces half-and-half

Directions

Freeze a highball glass for at least 30 minutes before serving.

Fill the glass with ice, add the vodka, orange juice, and half-and-half and stir.

When you are ready to eat, let the miracle berry tablet dissolve on your tongue and then enjoy the dish.

Replacing 2 teaspoons of sugar with the sweetness from the berry saves 32 calories per cocktail.

Kamikaze

Ingredients

Ice cubes

2 ounces vodka

¾ ounce freshly squeezed lemon juice

¾ ounce freshly squeezed lime juice

Directions

Fill a cocktail shaker halfway with ice. Add the vodka, lemon juice, and lime juice and cover tightly. Shake until the outside of the shaker is covered with frost. Strain over ice into a rocks glass.

When you are ready to drink, let the miracle berry tablet dissolve on your tongue and then enjoy the beverage.

Replacing 2 teaspoons of sugar with the sweetness from the berry saves 32 calories per cocktail.

ACKNOWLEDGMENTS

Anyone who has worked with me in the kitchen will tell you that I have a split personality when it comes to my work. One side is the joker—I want to have fun at work, and love playing involved pranks on my staff. The other side is a dead-serious entrepreneur who won't accept anything less than a perfect product. When it comes to inventing new dishes, cooking techniques, or innovating the way my restaurants operate, I push the limits. Of course, there are more failures than I'd like to admit, but my failures are what keep pushing me forward.

The only reason this book was possible is because some really brilliant people have contributed countless hours to this project. The environment I try to create with my staff is one in which everyone contributes and everyone benefits from our successes. I think it's the best workplace in the world. We all believe that collectively we can do something great.

Over the years, I have been approached to create a Moto cookbook, a how to re-create the restaurant's techniques at home . . . but I never felt compelled to do it. The only projects that excite me have to be tied to some aspect of social change. No matter how beautiful, a coffee table book doesn't exactly move you to change the way you cook or eat, or put a smile on your face after biting into a lemon that tastes like lemonade. When I started experimenting with the miracle berry, I realized the prankster in me as well as the social entrepreneur could join forces to create something important with this book.

The idea that a book like this has never been done before was very appealing. A lot of authors would like to make that claim, but with this book, it's a fact. Most modern recipes originated from other recipes, with a few tweaks of better or different ingredients. The cooking formulas haven't really changed in decades or even centuries. But cooking with an ingredient that is totally new requires different chemistry, which means every recipe in this book had to be tested and retested until it was perfect.

It takes a really special group of people to fully understand this. Every chef, every home cook, even my kids know that sugar makes food taste sweet. Imagine telling one of the best pastry chefs in the world to start cutting sugar from our desserts, but not use chemical-based sugar substitutes. Everything we use has to be natural, organic, and taste better than the original. I am pretty sure Ben Roche wanted to throw me in an oven. But we are still committed to these goals.

After my wife, Ben is probably the first person to tell me that I am crazy when I come up with one of my strange ideas. But after some finessing on my part, and a Jedi mind-trick or two, he eventually warmed up to the idea. It's one thing to eliminate sugar in simple homemade pastries, but to try to do it at a competitive high-end restaurant like Moto is just plain crazy.

Chris Jones was very instrumental in this project. While working at Moto, Chris oversaw all the menu items and made sure they are delicious. He quickly had to learn how to use acids to utilize the miracle berry's properties. At one point, he and I were consuming so much vinegar, lemon juice, and lime juice that our teeth began losing enamel. Fortunately, no one consumes dozens of lemons each day, but there were many times I wondered if this was ever going to work. Neither Chris nor I had ever written anything, and he had no experience in removing sugar from recipes, but he rose to the challenge. And more than halfway through the project, Chris got a call that changed his life forever. He was headed to Texas to compete on the ninth season of *Top Chef*. So just like that, my lead guy was out for more than two months.

When Chris left, Eric Marino stepped in. Eric was an intern at Moto who came back to work for us in the front of the house. He had a ton of experience with pastry, and agreed to assist in the recipe testing. He not only stepped in, he ran with it—and tested twenty recipes a day. His work was invaluable to this project.

Finally, I decided to get another chef to test all of the recipes with absolutely no guidance from me. That chef was Alexander Plotkin. Chef Plotkin had just returned from Copenhagen, where he worked with Chef René Redzepi in the lab at Noma Restaurant. He brought his talents to Chicago hoping to work as a research chef in the lab I am opening in 2012. He understood the level of simplicity needed for these recipes and worked tirelessly to make the recipes foolproof and easy to make at home, and I am so grateful for his part in this project.

My passion for the miracle berry wouldn't have amounted to much without

Charles Lee, the CEO of mberry. Without Charles's assistance, we would never have been able to experiment with the product as we have. We wouldn't have been able to open iNG Restaurant, which uses miracle berries in our flavor-changing menu. Before meeting Charles, I was paying $5,000 per kilo for freeze-dried miracle berry powder. When I told Charles about my dream to get rid of sugar and fight obesity with this book, he stepped in and made sure we had enough product to work with. Thanks, Charles. You are a real social entrepreneur and a valued friend.

My dear friend Paula Perlis was the spark that started it all. It was Paula who asked me to find a way to help a friend of hers going through chemo and radiation therapy. Her friend could only taste rubbery and metallic sensations and had lost all interest in eating. Paula asked me if I could find a way to bring her taste back. After weeks of chewing on tin foil and bike tires, Ben Roche and I found that this berry helped people who had lost their appetite enjoy food, and ultimately feel better. Today there are a number of controlled studies that have proven the berry's effectiveness with chemo and radiation patients, and Paula's dedication to this effort should be commended.

My wife, Katie, is the best home cook I know. She rolls her eyes at me when I say "home cook," thinking it's somehow less than a compliment. What I mean is, someone who takes the time and effort to prepare three healthy and homemade meals a day for her family, day in and day out, while also managing a full-time career, is a rock star. While Katie is my biggest fan, she had a lot of concerns about home cooks being able to incorporate the miracle berry into their home routine, so she started making the recipes at home. The true test was making the recipes for our daughters, Ella and Grace. At seven and five, they have their picky moments, but every time they ask me for a miracle berry for dessert, I know we are working in the right direction.

Finally, this book would not have happened without the support and assistance from my agent, Susan Ginsburg, and my editor, Jeremie Ruby-Strauss, who stepped in and really provided the direction needed for a useful book. Your help was invaluable.

INDEX

agave nectar, 7
almond paste, 258
amaretti cookies, chewy, 192
apple(s):
    baked, oatmeal, 33
    cardamom pie, 135–36
    cherry oat bars, 184–85
    crisp, 128–29
    pork with cider sauce and, 90–91
    puffed pancake, 20–21
    spice bread, 46–47
apricot chicken wings, spicy, 54
apricot-chipotle marmalade, 92–93
Asian short ribs, 98–99

banana:
    almond cookies, 205–6
    cream filling, 179–80
    nut muffins, 40–41
    -walnut spread, 259
beef:
    Asian short ribs, 98–99
    Korean, with quick kim chi and spicy
        sambal, 102–4
    and manchego empanadas, sweet and
        spicy, 61–63
    yellow curry, 100–101
berries, pavlova with, 218–19
blackberry ricotta tarts, 157–58
blueberry muffins, 38–39
blueberry pancakes, 18–19
brie en croûte, 52–53
brown butter-rosemary frozen custard,
    244
buttermilk substitute, 75–76
butternut squash risotto, sweet, 226–27
butternut squash soup, 64–65
butterscotch and lime custard, 162–63
butterscotch sauce, 163

cabbage: Southwestern coleslaw, 107–8
cakes:
    chocolate Guinness, 120–21
    crunchy polenta, with strawberries,
        118–19
    lemon poppy seed, with goat cheese
        frosting, 110–11
    molten chocolate, 124
    over-the-top lemon layer, 112–13
    pineapple zucchini, 116–17
    red velvet sheet, 122–23
    sticky toffee pudding, 164–65
    tres leches, 114–15
candied jalapeños, 106
cannoli, 220–21
caramel nut bars, 181–82
carrot cake whoopie pies, 177–78
champagne fizz to "lemon drop," 274
cheesecake bars, 188–89
cheesecake raspberry muffins, 36–37
cheese puffs, 50–51
cherry(ies):
    apple oat bars, 184–85
    chocolate coconut bars, 186–87
    chocolate ice cream, 235
    compote, 166–67
    fresh preserves, 253
    pop tarts, 26
    spiced jam, 257
chicken:
    kabobs with tamarind-date glaze, 82–83
    Marsala-less Marsala with parmesan pasta,
        80–81
    orange, 88–89
    roast, with 30-minute mole, 77–79
    rosemary, with corn bread stuffing, 74–76
    sesame, 84–85
    spicy apricot wings, 54
    teriyaki, 86–87

chocolate:
    buttercream frosting, 263
    cherry coconut bars, 186–87
    cherry ice cream, 235
    chocolate-chip ice cream, 233–34
    cocoa vodka, 277–78
    coconut oatmeal bars, 183
    -covered truffles, 212–13
    double, peanut butter pie, 151–52
    espresso cookies, 210–11
    fudge-striped spice cookies, 193–94
    Guinness cake, 120–21
    ice cream, 232
    martini, 277
    mocha frosting, 264
    molten, cakes, 124
    mousse, 159
    old-fashioned hot fudge, 251
    pots de crème, 160–61
    sour cream frosting, 262
    walnut torte with coconut crust, 125–26
cinnamon spice muffins, 42–43
cocktails, 271–86
coconut:
    chocolate cherry bars, 186–87
    chocolate oatmeal bars, 183
    crust, chocolate walnut torte with,
        125–26
    paneer with pineapple and, 228–29
coffee cake ice cream, 240–41
coffee granita, 248
coleslaw, Southwestern, 107–8
collard greens with ham hocks, 105
cookies:
    apple cherry oat bars, 184–85
    banana almond, 205–6
    caramel nut bars, 181–82
    cheesecake bars, 188–89
    chewy amaretti, 192
    chocolate cherry coconut bars, 186–87
    chocolate coconut oatmeal bars, 183

    chocolate espresso, 210–11
    cornmeal, 197–98
    date bars, 190–91
    fluffy oatmeal raisin, 209
    fudge-striped spice, 193–94
    iced pumpkin, 199–200
    Italian fig, 201–2
    jam thumbprint, 203–4
    lemon-thyme, 195–96
    pistachio, 207–8
corn bread, 74–76
cornmeal cookies, 197–98
crab Rangoon with orange dipping sauce,
    59–60
cranberry orange bread, 44–45
cream cheese frosting, 267
creamsicle (cocktail), 285
crepes, dreamsicle, 14–15
curry beef, yellow, 100–101
curry pork dumplings with sweet ginger garlic
    sauce, 55–56

date bars, 190–91
donuts, homemade, 29–30
dreamsicle crepes, 14–15

éclairs, lemon—cream cheese, 216–17
empanadas, sweet and spicy beef and
    manchego, 61–63

fig cookies, Italian, 201–2
French toast, 22–23
    baked, with raspberry syrup, 24–25
fruit, tropical, skewers with sweet yogurt
    dipping sauce, 127
fudge-striped spice cookies, 193–94

"gin and tonic" to sloe gin screw, 273
goat cheese frosting, 269
grape jelly, 254
grasshopper pie, 147–48

greyhound (cocktail), 283
Guinness chocolate cake, 120–21

ham hocks, collard greens with, 105
hot fudge, old-fashioned, 251

ice creams:
  brown butter-rosemary frozen custard, 244
  cherry chocolate, 235
  chocolate, 232
  chocolate chocolate-chip, 233–34
  coffee cake, 240–41
  coffee granita, 248
  margarita popsicles, 246
  pumpkin, 238–39
  strawberry balsamic, 236–37
  strawberry daiquiri popsicles, 245
  tiramisu, 242–43
  vanilla, 230–31
  watermelon sorbet, 247
Italian fig cookies, 201–2

jalapeños, candied, 106
jam thumbprint cookies, 203–4
jelly donut trifles, 214

kamikaze (cocktail), 286
key lime meringue pie, 141–42
Korean beef with quick kim chi and spicy
    sambal, 102–4

lemon:
  butter, 130–31
  buttercream frosting, 266
  -cream cheese éclairs, 216–17
  curd, 252
  lemonade tart, 139–40
  over-the-top layer cake, 112–13
  poppy seed cake with goat cheese frosting,
      110–11
  -thyme cookies, 195–96

lemon drop (cocktail), 276
lime dipping sauce, 228–29
lime-mint flan, 171–72

manchego and beef empanadas, sweet and
    spicy, 61–63
mango jam, 255
margarita, skinny, 275
margarita popsicles, 246
marmalade, apricot-chipotle, 92–93
Marsala-less chicken Marsala with
    parmesan pasta, 80–81
martini:
  chocolate, 277
  dirty, 279
mascarpone frosting, 268
mincemeat pie, 145–46
miracle berries, 3–4
  effects on foods, 5–6
  sources of, 4–5
  using, 5
mocha frosting, 264
mojito, 282
mole, 30-minute, roast chicken with, 77–79
muffins:
  banana nut, 40–41
  blueberry, 38–39
  cinnamon spice, 42–43
  raspberry cheesecake, 36–37

oatmeal, baked apple, 33
oatmeal raisin cookies, fluffy, 209
orange chicken, 88–89
orange meringue pudding, 168
orange waffles, 12–13

pad Thai, 70–71
pancakes:
  blueberry, 18–19
  puffed apple, 20–21
  spiced pumpkin, 16–17

paneer, homemade, 229
paneer with pineapple and coconut, 228–29
pasta, parmesan, Marsala-less chicken marsala
    with, 80–81
pavlova with berries, 218–19
peach bread pudding, 173–74
peach hand pies, 133–34
peach puffs, 215
peanut butter:
    and banana whoopie pies, 179–80
    double chocolate pie, 151–52
pear tarte tatin, 153–55
pickle juice, sweet, 261
pies:
    cardamom apple, 135–36
    double chocolate peanut butter, 151–52
    grasshopper, 147–48
    key lime meringue, 141–42
    mincemeat, 145–46
    peach hand, 133–34
    pumpkin, 143–44
    shortbread-topped strawberry, 137–38
    sweet crust, 132
piña colada, 281
piña colada pudding, 161
pineapple:
    paneer with coconut and, 228–29
    tarts, 155–56
    zucchini cake, 116–17
pistachio cookies, 207–8
polenta cake, crunchy, with strawberries, 118–19
pop tarts:
    cherry, 26
    dough, 28
    raisin nut, 27
pork:
    with apples and cider sauce, 90–91
    chops with apricot-chipotle marmalade,
        92–93
    curry dumplings with sweet ginger garlic
        sauce, 55–56

    pulled, sandwiches, 72–73
    ribs with BBQ sauce, 96–97
    tenderloin with prune-ancho barbecue
        sauce, 94–95
pots de crème, 160–61
pot stickers, shrimp, 57–58
pretzels, yogurt-covered soft, 224–25
prune-ancho barbecue sauce, pork tenderloin
    with, 94–95
puddings:
    butterscotch and lime custard, 162–63
    chocolate mousse, 159
    lime-mint flan, 171–72
    orange meringue, 168
    peach bread pudding, 173–74
    piña colada, 161
    pots de crème, 160–61
    rice, 175–76
    sticky toffee, 164–65
    Thanksgiving flummery with cherry
        compote, 166–67
    vanilla and thyme panna cotta with
        balsamic strawberries, 169–70
pumpkin cookies, iced, 199–200
pumpkin ice cream, 238–39
pumpkin pancakes, spiced, 16–17
pumpkin pie, 143–44

raisin nut pop tarts, 27
raisin nut spread, 260
raspberry:
    cheesecake muffins, 36–37
    icing, 270
    jam, 256
    rhubarb crostata, 149–50
    syrup, 24–25
red velvet sheet cake, 122–23
rhubarb raspberry crostata, 149–50
ribs with BBQ sauce, 96–97
rice pudding, 175–76
risotto, sweet butternut squash, 226–27